*for Doug Cameron
a True brother of the Light*

Making Light Of It

JAMES BROUGHTON

James Broughton

CITY LIGHTS BOOKS
San Francisco

© 1977, 1992 by James Broughton

Cover image by Joel Singer
Cover design by Rex Ray

James Broughton's films are available on 16mm from Canyon Cinema, 2325 Third St., San Francisco, CA 94107 and on video cassette from Facets, 1517 West Fullerton Ave., Chicago IL 60614.

Library of Congress Cataloging-In-Publication Data

Broughton, James Richard. 1913–
    Making light of it / by James Broughton. — 2nd rev. ed.
        p.   cm.
    Rev. ed. of: Seeing the light. 1977.
    ISBN 0-87286-265-8 : $7.95
    1. Motion pictures—Philosophy.   2. Motion pictures—Production and direction.   I. Broughton, James Richard. 1913–   Seeing the light. II. Title.
PN1995.B74   1992
791.43'01—dc20   92-2711
                                                                                        CIP

City Lights Books are available to bookstores through our primary distributor: Subterranean Company. P.O. Box 168, 265 S. 5th St., Monroe, OR 97456. 503-847-5274. Toll-free orders 800-274-7826. FAX 503-847-6018. Our books are also available through library jobbers and regional distributors. For personal orders and catalogs, please write to City Lights Books, 261 Columbus Avenue, San Francisco CA 94133.

CITY LIGHTS BOOKS are edited by Lawrence Ferlinghetti and Nancy J. Peters and published at the City Lights Bookstore, 261 Columbus Avenue, San Francisco, CA 94133.

To Joel, and all true brothers of the light.

There are pearls, but you must dive for them.

—Andrew Harvey

TABLE OF CONTENTS

Coming Into Focus 1

Film is a Way of Seeing 9

The Brotherhood of Light 15

Some Rules of the Game 29

Poetry in a Movie World 41

Zen in the Art of Cinema 47

The Oz of Cinema 63

Some Definitions 71

The Alchemy of Cinema 73

Some Fruits of Experience 85

Cinema and the Tao 87

Making Lights of My Own 95

Looking for a Future 117

Filmography/Bibliography 121

ILLUSTRATIONS

From *Together* (with Joel Singer), 1976 .... frontis

From *The Gardener of Eden*, 1981 viii

From *Mother's Day*, 1948 .... 4, 5

From *Four in the Afternoon*, 1951 .... 12, 13

From *Four in the Afternoon*, 1951 16

Directing *The Pleasure Garden*, 1953 20

From *The Pleasure Garden*, 1953 22

From *The Pleasure Garden*, 1953 28

From *The Bed*, 1968 37

From *The Bed*, 1968 38

From *The Golden Positions*, 1970 42

From *The Golden Positions*, 1970 43

From *The Golden Positions*, 1970 46

From *The Golden Positions*, 1970 .... 50, 51

From *Dreamwood*, 1972 58

From *Dreamwood*, 1972 61

From *Dreamwood*, 1972 62

Filming a scene, *Testament*, 1974 70

From the film *Erogeny*, 1976 84

Filming a scene, *Erogeny*, 1976 94

From *Devotions*, 1983 112

From *Devotions*, 1983 113

From *Testament*, 1974 120

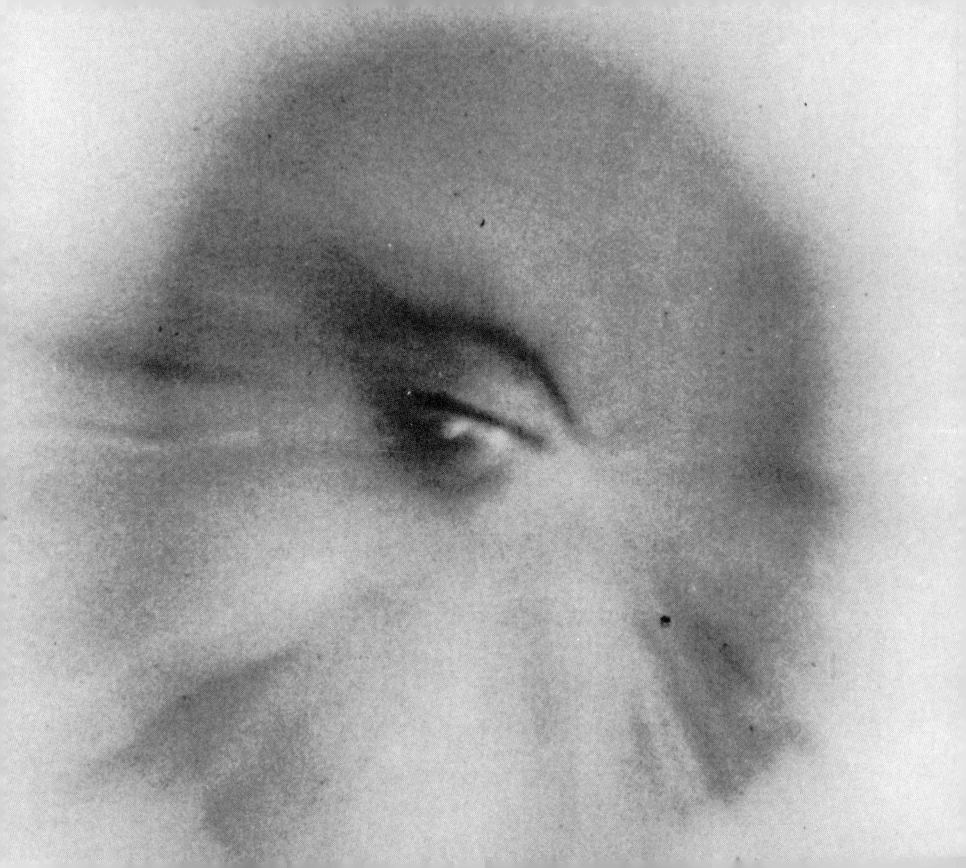

Coming Into Focus

> Beauty makes one lose one's head.
> Poetry is born of this decapitation
>
> —Jean Cocteau

On a foggy summer morning in 1946 Sidney Peterson took me to an abandoned cemetery in San Francisco where I discovered a new life. Along with us went a borrowed Cine Special 16mm camera, Army surplus black and white film, an aging actress in a nightgown and high heels, an adolescent poet with acne and warts, and a Kodak booklet entitled *How to Make Better Movies*. Thus began our filmmaking careers.

Neither Peterson nor I were sure of what we were going to do, or how far we might go with it, but we were determined to enjoy ourselves as inventively as possible. Surprisingly six months later the San Francisco Museum of Art premiered our finished film, touted as the "first surrealist film ever made in the Bay Area."

It did not matter that *The Potted Psalm* met with boos of bewilderment. We had learned the language of cinematography and most of its tricks. Incurably infected with filmic passion we were ready to go our separate ways. A year later I began my first solo film. This launched me on a journey spanning forty years in quest of a poetry that would reveal on a large screen what my feelings looked like.

Thanks to the press, Peterson and I came to be labeled fathers of a West Coast experimental film movement. Actually the decade of the forties saw a simultaneous flowering east and west with the first works of Maya Deren, Menken and Maas, John and James Whitney, and Kenneth Anger.

In the beginning we were called Experimental. Gradually we acquired other labels: Underground, Independent, New American, Alternative, Personal, Avant-Garde, Visionary. For my own work I prefer the term Poetic. By poetic cinema I do not mean fuzzy, fancy or bewildering. Personally I eschew blur. I love clarity, essence, sparkle. The virtue of the camera eye is its sharp and accurate focus. Isn't clarity the greatest of challenges? As Sigmund of Vienna says in *True & False Unicorn:* "Absolute Clarity is the mystery beyond."

For me cinema is not a history or a technology, it is an oracle of the imagination. For me cinema is poetry and love and religion and my duty to the Lords of Creation. I use these terms interchangeably. For me cinema involves delightments, incitements, enlightenments, and liberation machines.

I am not talking about films being good or bad. I am talking about the life of vision. I am talking about cinema as one way of living the life of a poet. I am talking about film as poetry, as philosophy, as metaphysics, as all else it has not yet dared to become.

Einstein said: "The most beautiful thing we can experience is the mysterious. It is the source of all true art and science."

Going to the movies, to indulge your fantasies or to have critical opinions, is certainly one way to pass your time. But it has little to do with the art of bringing the movie to life or bringing life to the movie. Be wary: life is what happens while you are doing something else.

"Try, as if you were one of the first men, to say what you see and experience and love and lose," wrote Rilke to a

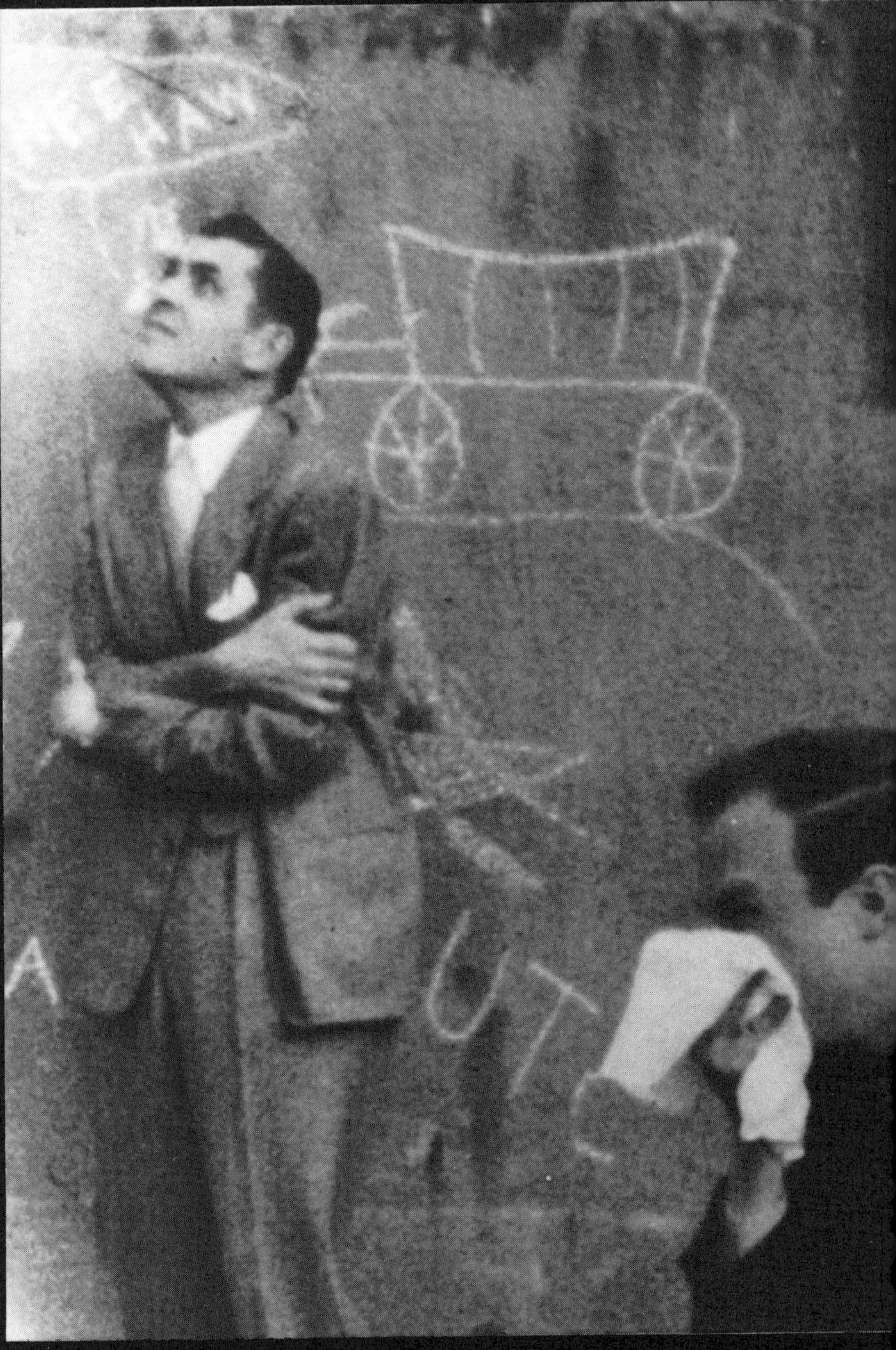

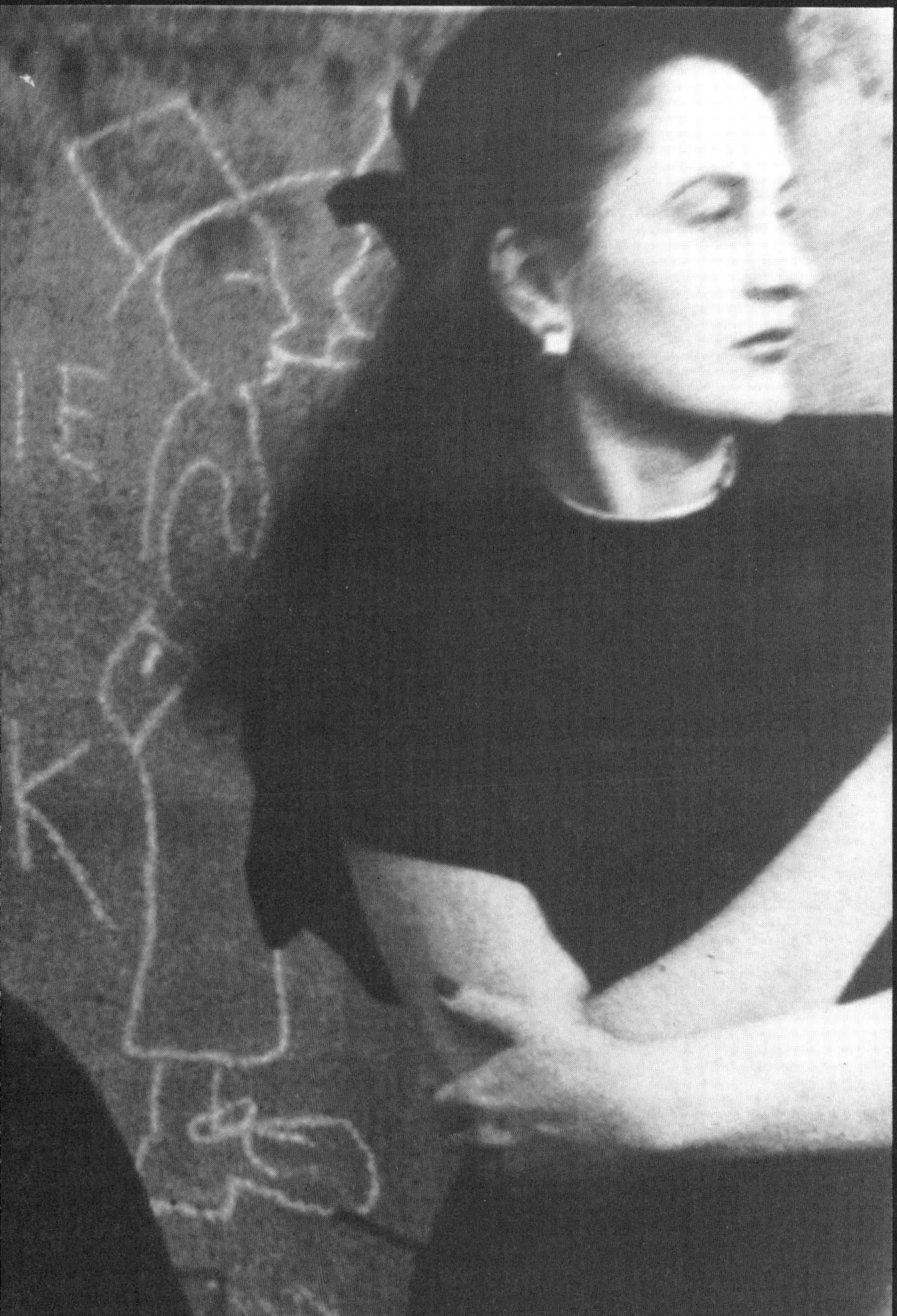

questioning young poet. Only thus will you discover your own peculiar angle to the universe, as Emerson called it.

True poets are as anarchic as Jesus and Lao-tzu. They particularly love revolutions, for revolutions are symbols of freedom from the major enemies of art: censors, critics, and collective inertia.

Every artist is in revolt. Because he is revolted by the passion for ignorance, greed and laziness in his fellow creatures. He knows a livelier realm where they might dwell, if only they could see the Light. So he tries to show them the Light. And they can't see it. They don't want to see it. They say, "I don't see anything in it." So he tries again. He lights another lamp, he foments another revolution.

But let us keep clear what kind of revolt we are talking about. Poets are not moral examples to society. Their value is in being obstreperous, outlandish, and obscene. Their business is to ignite revolutions of insight in the soul. Their duty is to shock a recognition in the mind.

Analytical theorizing is often felt to be "over one's head." It is nothing of the sort. It is in fact under one's feet. It is the mud one has to wade through: the bog of uncreative minds who build labyrinthine swamps of intellect to protect themselves from direct experience. What is truly over one's head is the realm of the poetic imagination. As Barnett Newman put it: "Aesthetics is for the artist as ornithology is for the birds."

So look up and look out and seek the Light that flies. When you travel, don't follow the main roads. Get lost. If you are too choosey about the spaces you visit, you may miss Inspiration Point.

Cinema like life is only worth living when it is in the service of something beyond the explicit and the mundane. When Marianne Moore was asked whether she wrote poetry for fame or for money, she replied, "Are there no other alternatives?"

Some years ago I came upon the following sentence (author unknown to me): "The purpose of life is to discover what the Glory of God is, and then to spend your life celebrating it." This banal sentence has kept me busy ever since. Such a view is not at all in fashion: nowadays we are encouraged to view the Glory of God as an anachronism. Secretly poets know better. However much they may grumble, they are enchanted by the epiphanies they discover, shape, or reveal.

We may not be able to alter our births and deaths, but we can render the interval between them more endurable. And even transcendent. "Where your bliss is, that is where your god dwells." Then, as St. Augustine advised, "Love God, and do what you will." In fact, do not think about God at all, but experience *being* God.

Jung said the sole purpose of human existence is to kindle a light in the darkness of being.

So, let there be some light. Do you see the Light? Do you seek the Light?

Do you have a film in front of your eyes? Or do you have a film over your eyes?

The Light, said Paracelsus, is the star within us. Bring forth your own light, however dimly it glows.

Besides stars, meteors, and lightning there are flashlights, hurricane lamps, matches, birthday candles, sparklers, bonfires, and pilot lights.

I Thessalonians 5:5 says: "Ye are all the children of light."

Seek, penetrate, magickize! Radiance is the nature of the Divine.

Film is a Way of Seeing

> The seat of the soul is where the outer and inner worlds meet.
>
> —Novalis

Film is a way of seeing. It is not mere looking. It may lead to vision. But these three ways are not the same way.

People look at art. They very seldom see it. They read the labels.

One can look at something until one ultimately sees it, but this is very rare. Most people don't even look. They need films to show them what to look at, otherwise they would not realize the wonder of faces, places, and the surprises of the ordinary.

Art is a way of seeing the unseen and the unnoticed, the unseeable and the unacknowledged. The basis of all poetry is the fresh stare. Critics object when they are not shown what they expect to see. Intellect cannot believe that the universe is a warm and changeable thing.

When one can respond without preconceptions then vision can occur. Then one can say, "I see." Because then one has met an illumination.

Film is a way of seeing, of seeing life happen, of seeing what happens to life. Film is a way of seeing what has been looked at by everyone and never really seen.

Vision is a way of seeing how life triumphs over all distinctions and pronouncements, such as these of mine.

Insist on your own eye. Insist on your own seeing. Insist on yourself. No matter how odd you look, or how oddly you see. Every morning be newly enlightened by the sun. Unless you are a night watchman or an owl-catcher full daylight sets the norm of your vision. Measure insight in terms of the roar of day and you will be at the center of the planetary dance.

Light the lights. Light the way to sights and insights. Don't settle for tiny flashes and dim wits. Things are shady enough as they are. Open your eyes to the farthest point you can imagine.

Seek the light within things as well as what shines upon them. Reveal the radiance within every human and every act of being.

Be addicted to experiment and wonder. Surrender to what possesses you. Discard whatever stymies your flexibility. The creative mind plays with the object it loves.

Filmmaking is traditionally spoken of as an activity of shooting. If this is your occupation, aim at being a sharpshooter. Don't shoot the breeze or shoot the works. Shoot straight and love the target. A crack shot is neater than a shot in the dark.

Let your dreams find you and kick you out of bed. Be a passionate curiosity, not a body of information. Be a bloodhound sniffing buried treasure. A hound doesn't talk theory. Ida P. Rolf said, "Don't try to figure it out, let your fingers find it."

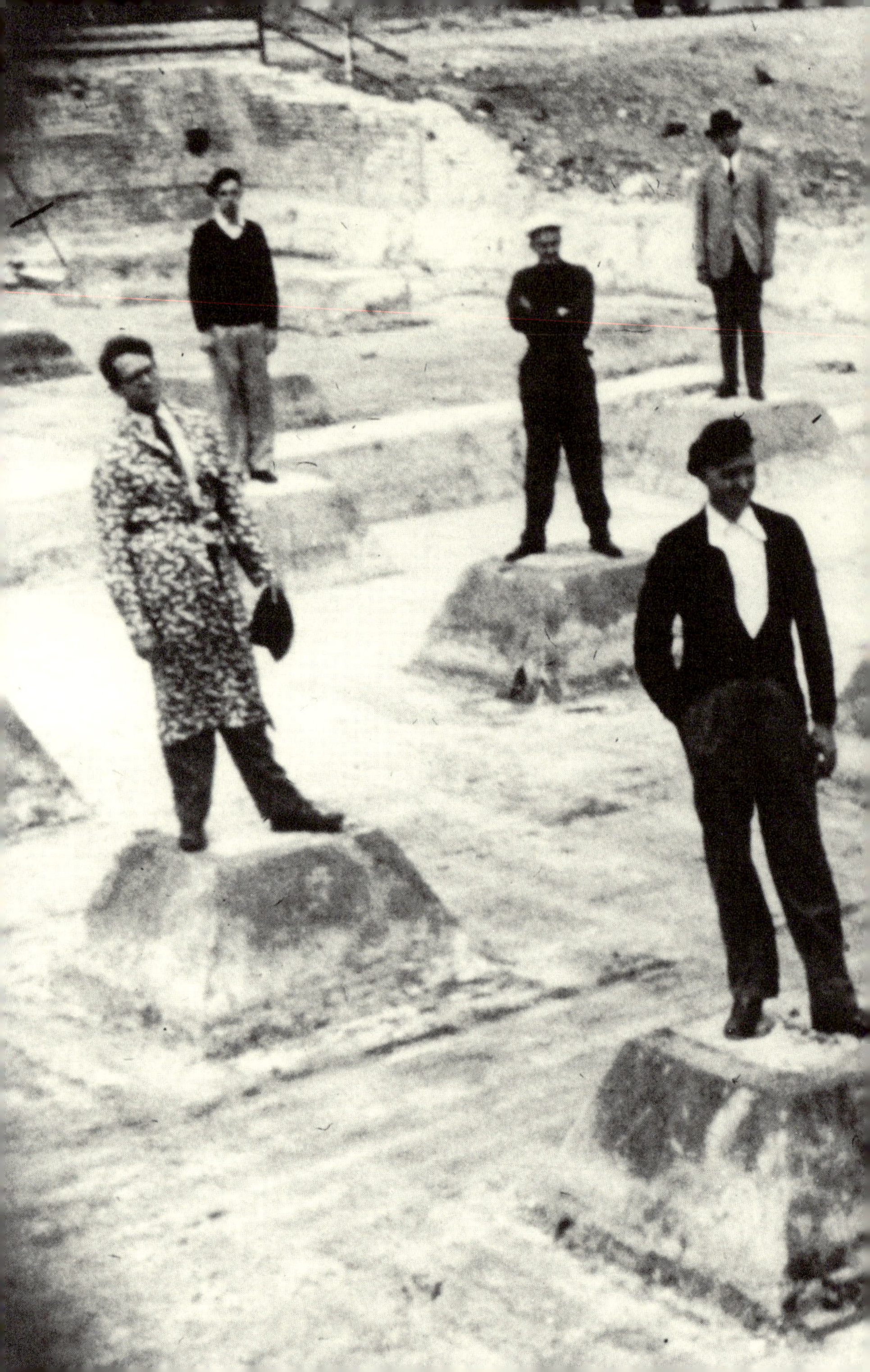

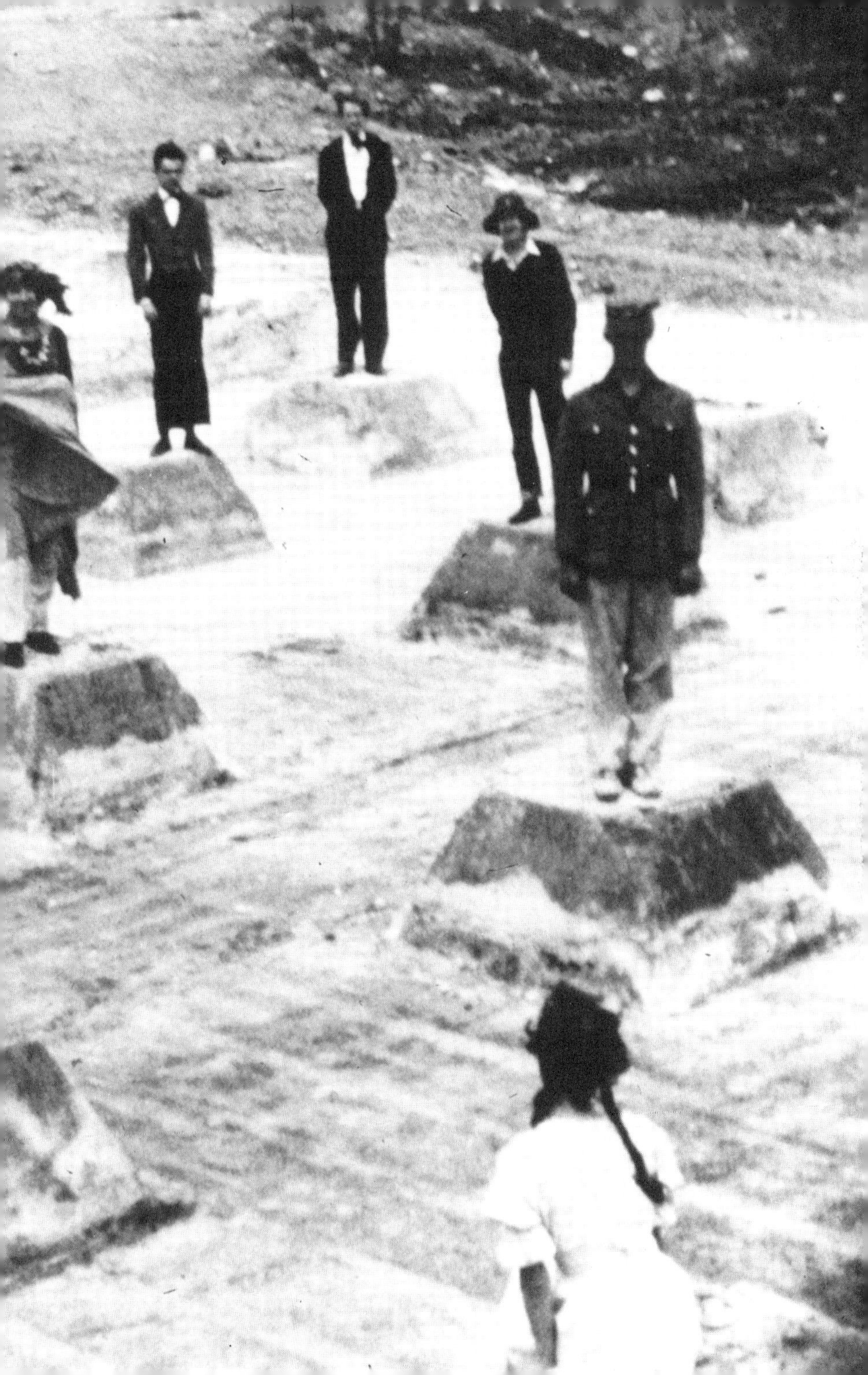

From the brink of not knowing dive into the unknown. Trust your rip cord. It is the only way to discover what you do know. Be ready for belly-flops and for booby traps, but don't criticize your flights. You can't stop in midair to revise a swan dive. To practice what you know may take a lifetime.

The Brotherhood of Light

> If you don't live it, it won't come out of your horn.
>
> —Charlie Parker

Do you want to make a personal film? Want to bring your visions to life? Warning: a visionary film is a dangerous quest. Will you promise to make visible the invisible, express the inexpressible, speak of the unspeakable? Do you know how to go about it? Do you know where it will lead you?

I can tell you what I know, or think I know, about the making of poetic cinema and the poetry of making cinema. I am not an expert on anything, but I have been a poet shaped by movies since childhood and during the past forty years I have tried to express some of my own visions on film. It's possible that the very next work I attempt may disprove my knowledge. Every new film

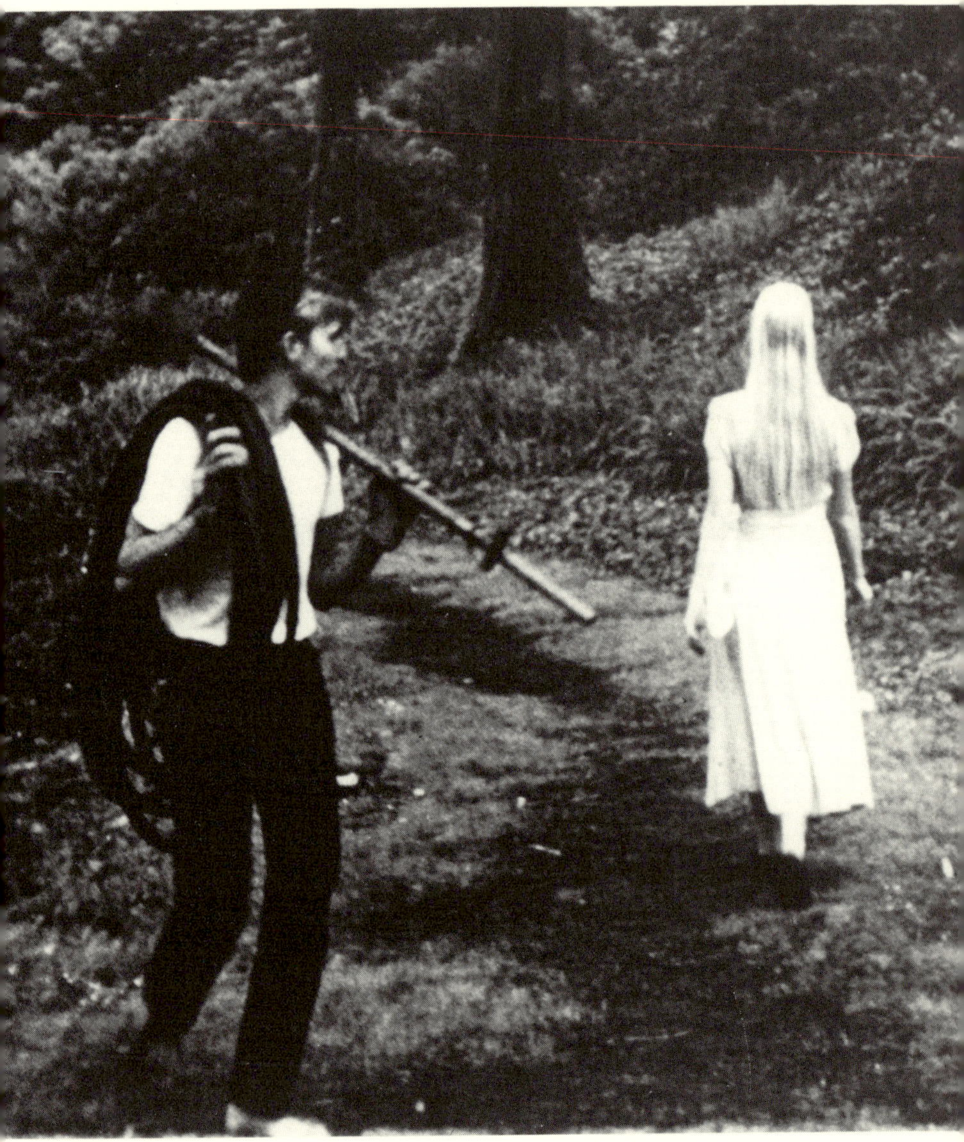

begins from scratch, from a roll of blank film, as if one knew nothing at all. Another leap in the dark, another jump off a cliff!

So I do not claim to be right about my own pronouncements. As the old sage Lao-tzu said, no one can be right without also being wrong. Nor do I have any pretension that I am saying anything new. Wisdoms are clichés; the best ones are great clichés. I set down my own true isms in the form of precept and admonition for the very good reason that they comprise what I repeatedly advise myself. But if you are a true poet you will pay no attention to good advice. You will make your own mistakes in your own peculiar way and so discover your own view of the world.

What is a visionary? Fellini has answered: "For me, the only realist is the visionary because he bears witness to his own reality."

THE INITIATION: SOME ELEMENTARY QUESTIONS

Has your angel touched you on the shoulder and told you that you must risk all?

Do you believe that you are one of those who must serve the true god of cinema?

Are you willing to live in the dedicated service of the Great Projector?

Are you like the child who cried out on waking, "Turn on the light! I want to see my dreams!"?

Do you long to see your own images cast before the world in a beam of light?

Making a film is a more hazardous act than looking at one. For you will create a dream. Whereas dreams themselves are natural events which happen to us. You will make a dream happen for others to dream with and be dreamed by.

Every film is a voyage into the unknown. You set out for Cathay and arrive at a very small island in the Caribbean. You will need to drag your crew through storms and famine, keep them from mutiny, keep them from suspecting your own doubts. And sometimes, once you have arrived, they will claim the credit and the spoils.

If you don't particularly care for Columbus, would you settle for Vasco da Gama? Magellan? Neil Armstrong? What explorer can cross uncharted seas without a passionate faith in his vision of the treasures he will discover? This is an attitude toward life, and its ship flies the flag of the poet.

I have never begun a film, however well prepared, that did not prove to have a life of its own and lead me to a region where I did not expect to go. What safaris! What narrow escapes! The maps can lead directly to quicksands and the jaws of dragons. Yet sometimes the end of the trail may be quite near El Dorado.

It is not we who play with cinema. The nature of cinema plays with us. Your film knows better than you what form it wants to have, what corners it wants to turn, and what its real meaning is. Let it take you wherever it wants to go. Nietzsche's cry was: Live dangerously! Which is the same thing as: Live poetically!

Well, are you ready? Are you willing to be initiated?

It is unwise to embark on the high seas without knowing a few of the laws of navigation. To have a shipwreck before you have cleared port is both messy and embarrassing. Try to get out to the open sea before you attempt to sink or swim.

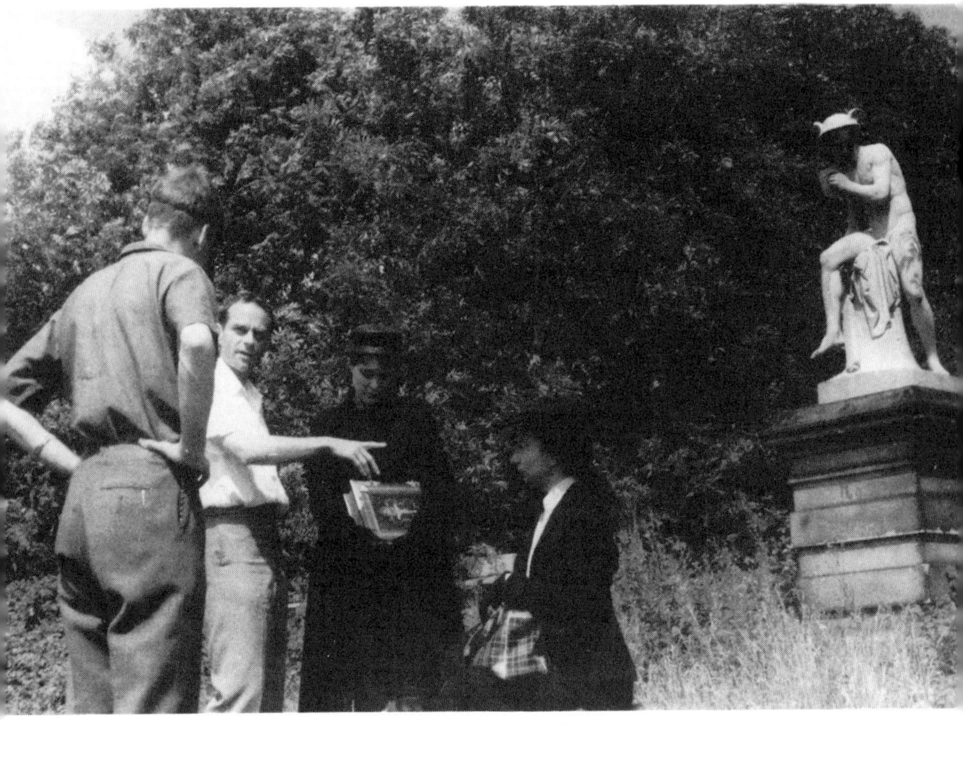

Let's begin with a little catechism.

First of all, do you believe in Light?

Do you seek the Light? Are you entranced by the Riddle of Lumen? Does the darkening hall give you an expectation of mysteries to be revealed?

Does the sound of a projector and the flicker of focus leader set your nerves into eager anticipation?

Are you willing to accept Illumination as the true faith?

Do you want to be enlightened? Do you want to be enlightening? Do you want to join the Order of the Brothers of Light, founded in 1895 by two French brothers aptly named Lumière?

I speak in ecclesiastical terms, not out of frivolity, but to emphasize the seriousness of the way of life you will have to live once you have taken the vows.

If you consider cinema to be the super art of our century, its iconography unveiled before theater congregations around the world, then it is a calling to be embraced in responsible and solemn terms.

At one and the same time we must ask the best of ourselves and of cinema itself.

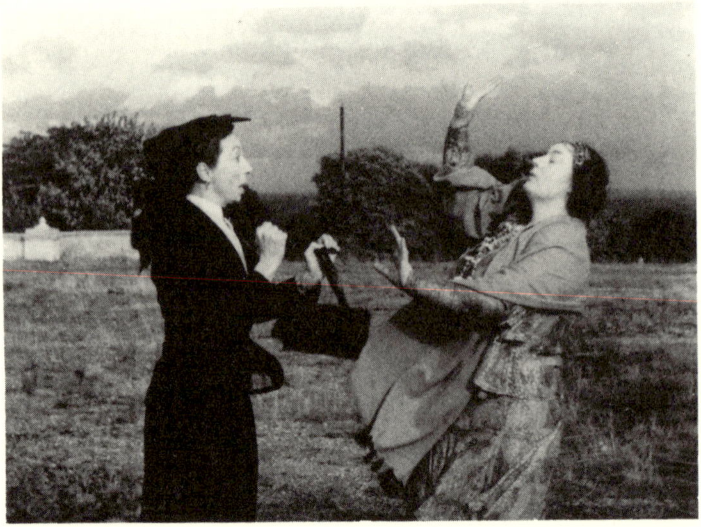

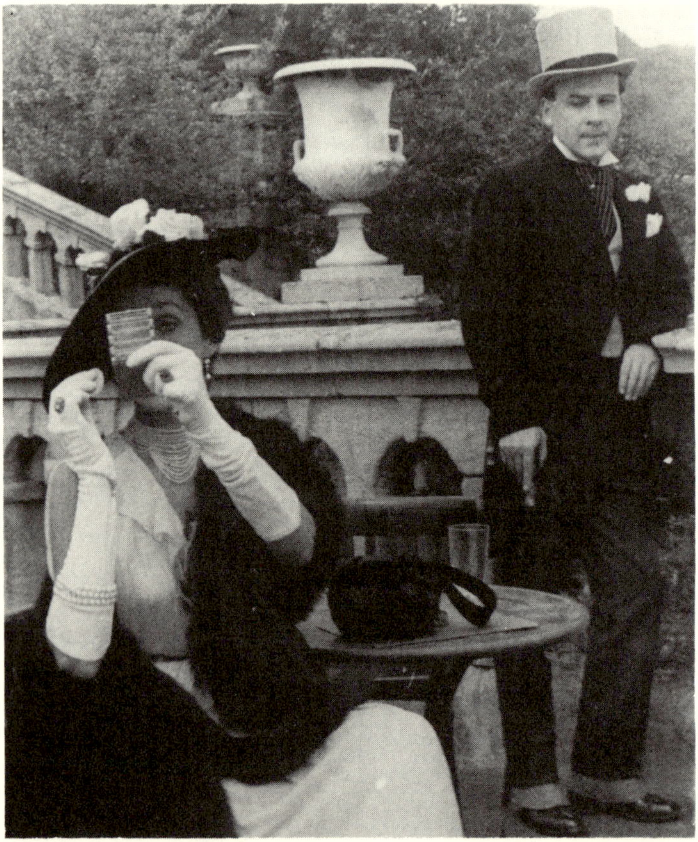

Interlude: a short hymn, entitled
"The Secret Name of Cinema is Transformation":
    Transform transform
    anything everything—
    stairways into planets
    navels into buttercups
    icebergs into elephants—
    everything
    everywhere
    the old scene renewed by seeing
    the unseen seen anew
    transformed

THE PREPARATION

Before you can be accepted as novice into the Brotherhood of Light, you must first renounce the world and its works. Specifically, the doctrines of the orthodox non-believing fathers: producers, distributors, exhibitors, critics, promoters, hacks, academics, executives, professional moviemen, and all those who look upon acts of vision as a form of heresy. They are easily terrified by visual phenomena, by self-revelation, by the glory of creation, by anything touched with an artist's own hand. Have no traffic with them. They are the devil's agents who will tell you that you are mistaken, misguided, misbegotten, and a miserable misfit. Don't bother trying to enlighten them. Save your breath and slam the door. They are the enemies of art.

"If all men lead mechanical unpoetical lives, this is the real nihilism, the real undoing of the world, to which Dante's Hell is but a fairy story," said R. H. Blyth in *Zen and Zen Classics*.

Fortunately the Brotherhood of Light is an order wherein the joy of creation reigns and where the agonies of cinema lead to the pleasures it reveals.

THE VOWS

Are you ready and willing to take the Three Vows—the vows of Poverty, Chastity, and Obedience?

Poverty: because you will be forever in debt to the camera store and the laboratory, and will be forever begging from friends and foundations.

Chastity: because you will be wedded to your work and your wildest escapades will be with it.

Obedience: because your life will be in the service of an endlessly demanding tyrant with more heads than a hydra and more legs than a centipede.

And what is the reward for following these vows? Nothing. Nothing but the joy of serving the gods. Nothing but the satisfaction of losing your shirt and finding your bliss.

THE CREDO

And now it is time to learn the Credo. Let us sing in unison:

I believe in the camera, the lens, the filter, the tripod, and the meters of all light.

I believe in the reflector, the quartz lamp, the charges of batteries, and the recording powers of all equipped things.

I believe in the reel, the film stock, the emulsion, and in all the possible pictures of earth and heaven.

I believe in twenty-four frames per second, the single frame as an atom of time, and all possible metric durations of image.

I believe in the cut, the splice, the A and B roll, the optical printer, and the superimposition of all things.

I believe in the union of light and darkness, the conjunction of sound and silence, and the projection of these in all times and places.

Furthermore, I believe in the Brothers Lumière, Méliès the Magicker, Our Father Griffith, Sergei the Eisenstein, Carl the Dreyer, Jean the Coctelian, Sts. Von and Von, St. Buster, St. Charlie, and all the other ascended masters and their good works. And in the community of avant-garde saints I believe in St. Deren the Beatified, St. Mekas the Evangelist, and St. Brakhage the Redeemer.

THE PLEDGE

I swear to abstain from all ready-made ideas and from all critical assumptions.

I swear to refrain from falling in love with my own footage.

I swear to be precise, ruthless and articulate.

I swear to delight the eye and ear of all creatures.

I swear to attempt the impossible, to exceed myself, and to venture where no one has ever pushed a button before.

I swear that my aim will always be: to put the right image in the right place at the right time and at the right length.

Here ends the ritual of initiation for the Brothers of Light. The lesson is simple. There are only two commandments on which hang all the loss and the profits: Love thy cinema with all thy heart and with all thy soul and with all thy mind. And love thy fellow filmmaker as thyself.

Now let us pause for our own commercial. "Wine, music, and cinema are the three great creations of humanity," said one T'Ian, a cultural spokesman for Chairman Mao.

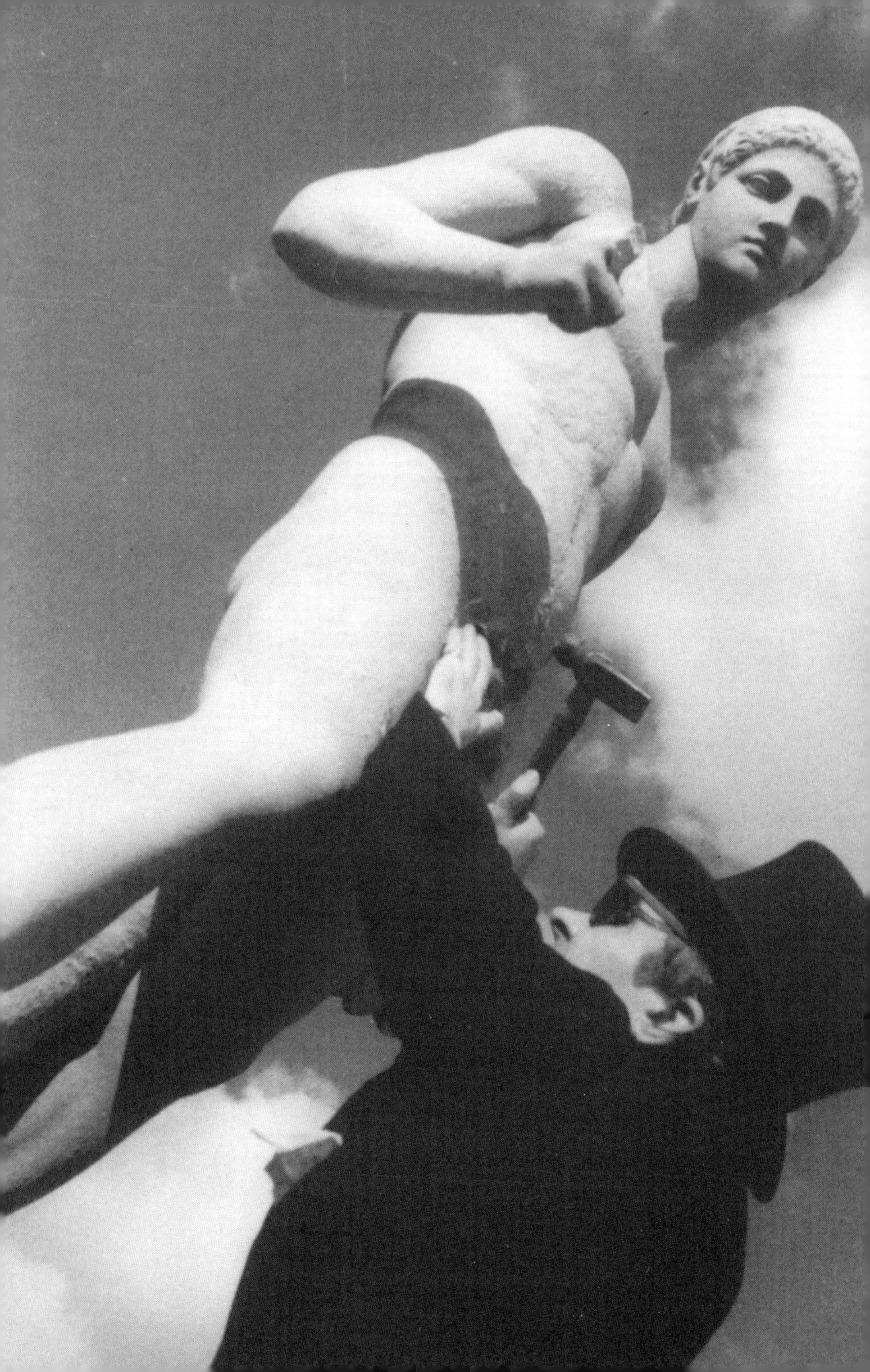

Some Rules of the Game

> A combination of words and music with color and movement can extend human experience in a way that words alone cannot do.
>
> —Kenneth Clark

The task remains crashingly simple and endlessly difficult: Explore! Visualize! Articulate!

Degas said, "A picture is something which requires as much knavery, trickery, and deceit as the perpetration of a crime."

Start with light. And delight. Take delight in. Take delight in what is here and what is now. And look at it. And take the light in. And light it. With the delight of light. And the light of delight.

You are a window between the beholder and the beheld. The secret password is: translucence.

Above all you must be a lover. A lover of sights and sounds. Then you must learn to focus lovingly. By which I mean: pay attention, be alert, stretch your senses, be mindful of everything. Learn all the rules so that you will know which ones you have to break.

It is not of camera operation alone that I am speaking. Almost any idiot can learn in a short time how to run a machine. But the more you know about everything besides cinema the better your cinema will become. The more richness of experience you bring to every set-up the better it will set up. The more you know firsthand of painting, poetry, theater, music, color and design, history, dance, geography, architecture, myth, psychology, magic, and the other realms of human articulation, the sturdier your film will stand.

You may be reeking of talent, but real art comes from knowledge. No work can be greater than the man who makes it.

So what will your film be about? It can be about anything. But what do *you* care most about?

Stick to your deepest concerns. Don't try to do everything. Debussy found his style by using only those notes that he liked. What are you obsessed by? What haunts your private hours? What do you discover when you enter your own mirror? Tell us, show us! What is going on in the secret chambers of *your* Hôtel des Folies-Dramatiques?

Don't waste your time making a film like anyone else's. That's duplication of effort. Besides, it won't be any good. Your business is to make something that neither you nor I have ever seen before. Your business is to make a wonderful new kind of mess in your own way.

If it doesn't fit into any recognizable category for the festivals and the critics, that's too bad. About them. When you have made your own room, room will have to be made for you. Forget about critics. Don't adopt their values or adapt to them. You are not an arbiter of taste. Your business is to be your own man or woman. Your business is to take the risk of your madness. Say hello, Rimbaud.

Excellent strategy: do what you are most afraid of doing. Look what Brakhage did. He had always feared death, it had been a constant threatening imminence for him. So, with the courage that has always made him a trailblazer, he took his camera firmly in hand and went into the city morgue of Pittsburgh, looked closely and filmed unforgettably the forms of death as they had never been seen before: *The Act of Seeing With One's Own Eyes*.

Live on the edge! Are you just playing around? What are you saving yourself for? Live as if every day were your last!

When I made my first film I thought seriously that it would be the only film I would ever make. *Mother's Day* was not made to please anyone but myself. It was done out of absolute necessity: to discover what my inner haunting looked like. I accepted it as my first and last chance, a one and only shot: I risked everything. All work should be approached that way. Still today every film I make is my "last."

What does it matter whether *Mother's Day* was influenced by *Blood of a Poet*, *The Andalusian Dog*, or *Meshes of the Afternoon*? That sort of thing is only a critic's means of putting you in your place (or some other place where you can be filed away) so that your uniqueness can be discounted.

What if I admitted that my film aesthetically owes much more to my grandmother's family album, to landscapes of de Chirico, music of Stravinsky, and verses of Mother

Goose than it does to anything in film history? Or, what if I acknowledged that the major influence came from the traumas of my childhood that I carried in my heart for twenty years before I ever began filmmaking? Godard, in *La Chinoise:* "Art is not a reflection of reality. It is the reality of a reflection."

When I made *The Bed* at the request of Jacques Ledoux I thought it would be a one and only last shot. *The Bed* has no special style, there isn't a trick in it, it is all straight cuts. I wanted to reveal as directly as possible my vision of the endless dance of human existence. I thought of it as a private communication to an old friend in Brussels. The public success of the film astounded me.

Don't think about success, no matter how famous you want to be. Success is out of your hands. That is what other people do with your work. It will happen if it happens, you can't force people to like you. Your business is the achievement: the best you are capable of, however eccentric.

Don't make anything with the desire to impress anybody. You are more apt to depress them. Make it to share your delight, to expose your pain. Make it to please yourself or a friend or a beloved. Make it to the Glory of God. Maybe one or two strangers will share your illumination.

Poetry is an act of love, it asks no rewards. Remember the caution of Castañeda's Don Juan: "Does this path have heart?"

Honor your dreams. The gods visit you in your dreams. C. G. Jung carved over his front door: "The gods are always present, even if uninvited."

Love your dreams! Expand your dreams!

In Jungian therapy there is a practice called Active Imagination. In this you are urged to spin off with a dream you have had, letting it unravel however it wants to: in other words, dreaming awake.

How active is your own imagination? How far do you let it go? For Blake imagination was the star in man. There are many less rewarding pursuits than following a star.

If you become familiar with your dreams, you will enter the translucent realm of the archetypes, those potent primal images of mankind. They contain much more excitement than topical events.

Let me quote Jung again: "He who speaks in primordial images speaks with a thousand voices, he enthralls and overpowers, while at the same time he lifts the idea he is trying to express out of the occasional and the transitory into the realm of the ever-enduring."

Images that grow from our roots to shape the future of mankind are the ones to cherish. The images that you make public become your own mythology and part of the destiny of all men. Dahlberg said it: "Be primordial or decay!"

"Follow your own Weird." But this doesn't mean that all you have to do is turn on the camera and express yourself. Just as talking has nothing to do with creating, self-expression has nothing to do with art. "Anything goes" may be therapy but that is only prelude to the shaping of what has been unloosed. For a painter the frame defines the shape of the image. A filmmaker must work within the fixed rectangle of the camera eye. Ideally this limitation focuses his imagination.

A word about being original. In a word: don't worry about it. A new technique, a new gimmick, is not automatically a new vision. Originality has nothing to do with novelty. The word comes from origin. Thus your original nature is in your roots. As the Zen koan asks, "What was your original nature before you were conceived?"

Many kinds of clever cinema flourish. Some of it is genuinely innovative, some of it is exhilarating exercise for the eyes. But most of it is what Kubelka called "festival kitsch."

Keep true to your own nature and you will be original enough. Trust your feelings, intuitions, assumptions, attitudes, and follies. Go deep. Don't wrestle with a mouse. Exercise an angelic foe or a challenging daimon.

A Zen poem says, "If you do not get it from yourself, where will you go for it?"

If you want to be avant-garde, never do what the avant-garde is doing. By the time everybody knows what's new, it's wearing an old hat. The true scout of the vanguard is already far out of town, exploring a fresh wilderness. Michelangelo: "He who follows will never advance."

The avant-garde task is to deal with what nobody else is attending to. This keeps widening human consciousness and maintains balance in the universe.

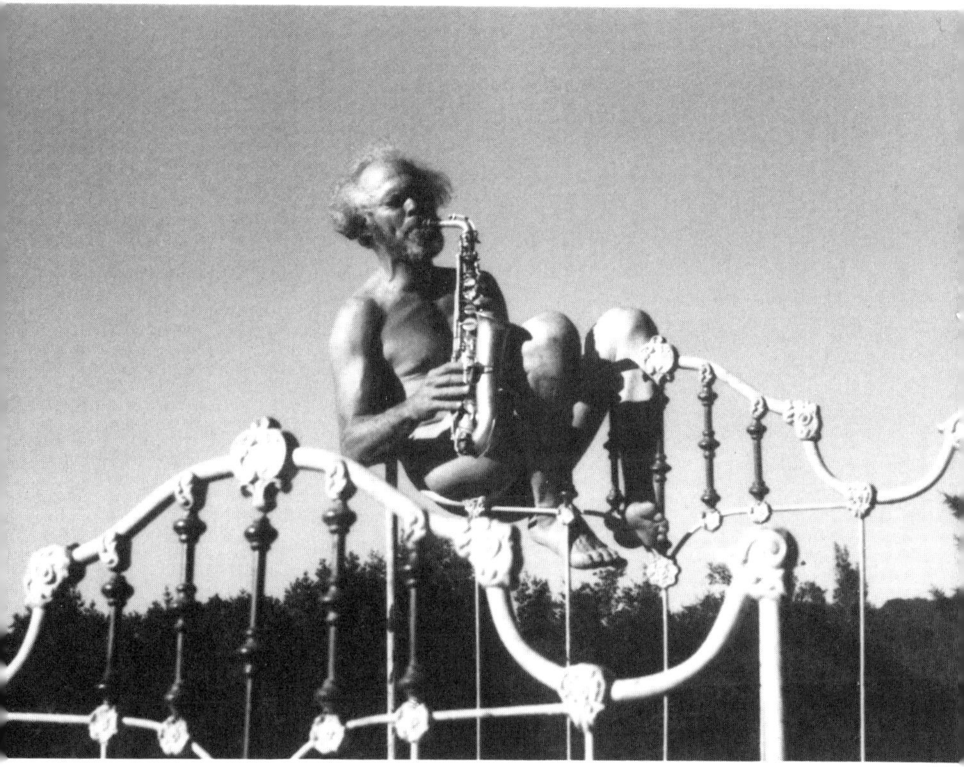

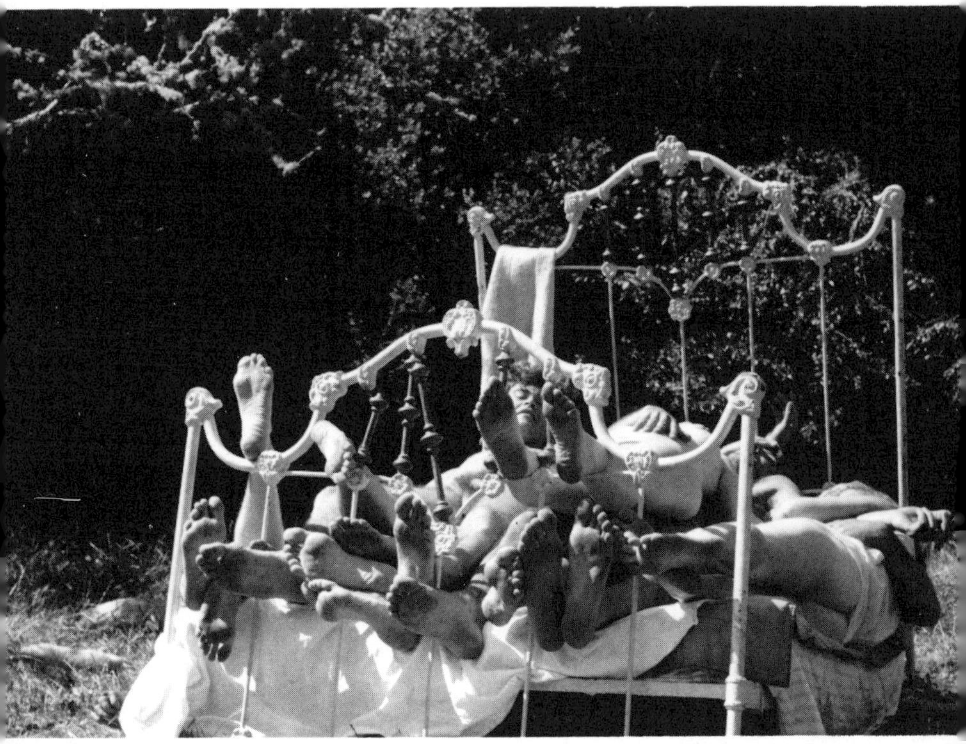

As for the form to give your vision, the surest way to look avant-garde is to revitalize an old form. "There is nothing new but what has been forgotten." Look at all that Picasso dug up. "Make it New" was Ezra Pound's motto, and that's what he did with Provençal, Chinese, Anglo-Saxon forms. *The Golden Positions* looked "new" because I went back to Muybridge.

Perhaps the ultimate avant-garde position: to reach the place where you no longer lean on any object, any reference. Or what Krishnamurti called "the stairway without any railing." Then you might reach the sphere of the innate light, the Mother Light, the light of which all other lights are the children.

Can you push beyond your dreams to the pure light of dreaming?

For the Brothers of Light Cinema is:
    a form of yoga discipline
    a service of prayer and thanksgiving
    a translucent mystery
    a devotional agony
    a quest for ecstasy
    a new creation of the world

a society of explorers
a fellowship of the inner radiance

There is a lady in Firbank's novel, *Vainglory*, who shivers ecstatically at the prospect of being memorialized in a stained glass window: "Oh to be pierced by light!"

Poetry in a Movie World

> While we are here
> living an illusion,
> let us regale ourselves in it.
>
> —Michael McClure

Is cinema our mystery religion?

Group movements of the soul have usually involved dramatic ritual: the coliseum, the cathedral, the bullring, the theater. For us, the movies.

One enters the darkened place and joins the silent congregation. Like Mass, performances begin at set times. You may come and go but you must move quietly and with respect. Up at the altar space a rite is to be performed in which you are expected to participate.

Then out of the shadows comes the beam of light: the Projector, the Great Projector up there behind us!

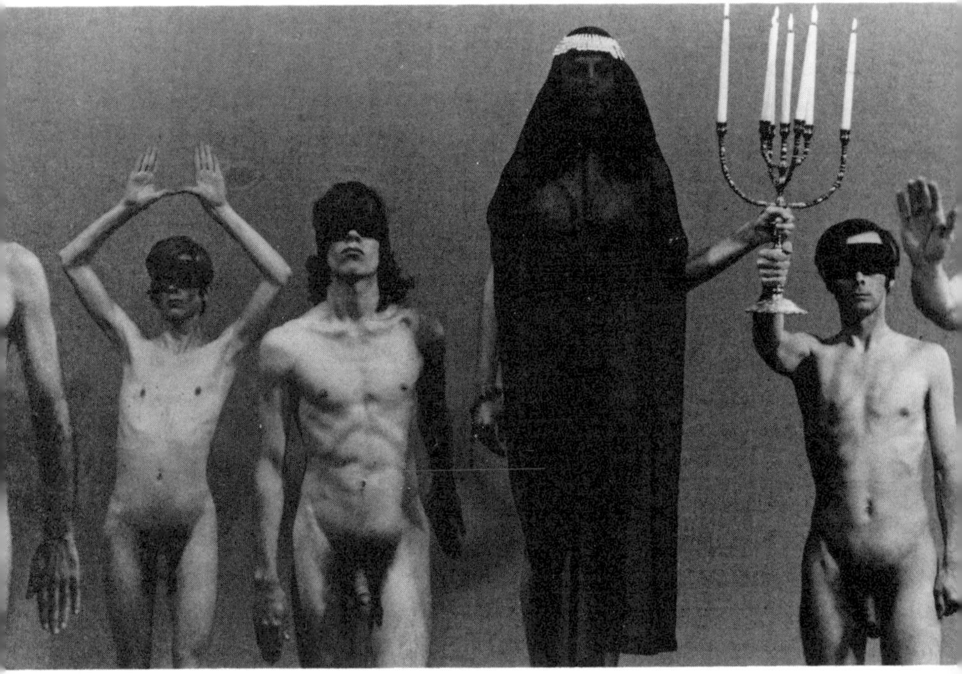

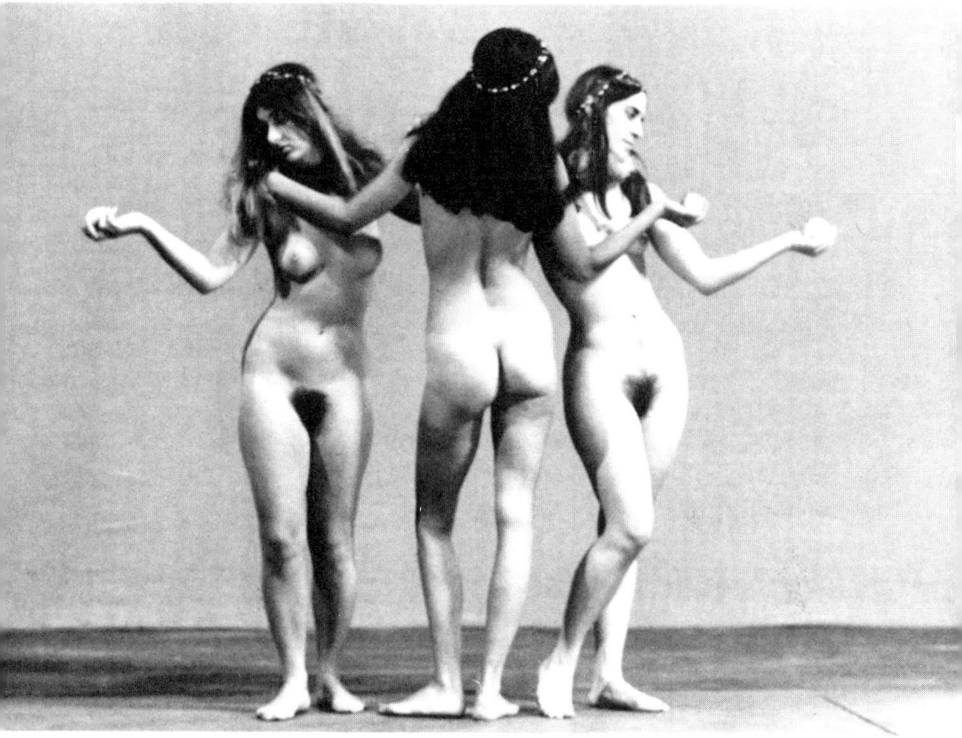

Turn out the little lights so that the big light can penetrate the darkness!

Behold the unreeling of the real and unreal reality of practically everything: dreams, idiocies, and disasters; our nativity, passion, and death.

Film is the contemporary art because it moves in time as our lives do, and its eyes can go everywhere. It does not have to be a total picture at once like the easel painting. It is a total only after it has been added up.

Unlike a book in your hand a film keeps on going whether you like it or not. For it has an existence of its own. A microcosm larger than life, its boundaries are boundless.

Modern poetry has been deeply influenced by film. Modern film has seldom returned the compliment.

Poets have to be contemporary. Otherwise they might as well take up taxidermy. Poetry lives now in a movie world. When will the movie world live with poetry? Cinema may be the most modern of the arts, but it tends to be prosy and conservative.

To ask for poetry in cinema does not mean that one is asking for more talk: the movies talk too much as it is. Rather, one is asking for essences. For cadence, ouch, and absurdity. For how we really feel and dream. Away with the diet of second hand! Fresh eyes, personal vision, imagination made fact! Genuine love, death, and folly, not Mme. Tussaud's.

To ask for poetry in film does not mean that one is yearning for High Art. Nor talking about Great Films. Simply a fresh vision, a key opening a door.

It is easier to be pretentious than to be at ease. It is easier to make great confusion than it is to create a simple complicated truth. One asks merely for a little magic. If the magician's act turns out to be Great Art, that part of it will not be his concern. The unforgettable films remain those conceived with the sturdiest poetic imagination.

Like a film, a poem is intended both to be looked at and to be heard. It is both image and language, vision and music. It has movement and form, a progression and a meaning. And it is to be remembered, and looked at again.

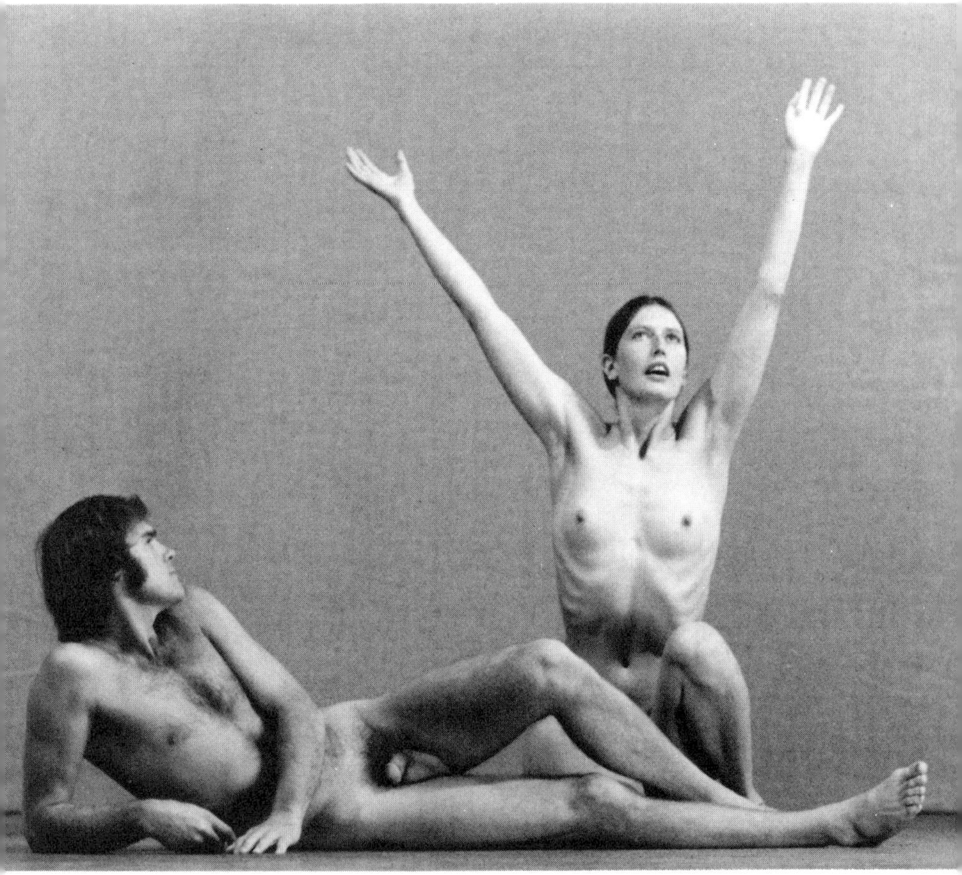

Zen in the Art of Cinema

> When logics die
> The secret grows through the eye.
>
> —Dylan Thomas

Art is a quest for freedom and Zen is a good way to prepare for the quest. The woods are certainly full of more misleading alternatives. Everywhere mules palmed off as gazelles! Zen remains one of the great poetic disciplines of the world.

Zen is usually identified as being unidentifiable. So you can make up your own definition. For Zen means not being enslaved by any point of view. Zen is not a religion or a philosophy or a theory or a church. It is a poetic way of life. Zen knows the mind is not to be relied upon in crucial matters. (I make my own Zen as I make my own Oz or my own Christianity. If you swallow bodies of thought whole, you can choke on dogmas.)

The true way of discovery is intuition: the poetry's archery.

> He who knows that flowers are visions
> let him enter boldly
> —Guido

Nobody can tell you what Zen is, but it's not hard to find out what you do with it.

First of all, you sit. You start your day with sitting and you end your day with sitting. Zenites practice zazen on zafus in a zendo. That's the way you put your mind quietly into your bottom. In solemn circles this is called meditation. Meditation is emptying your mind of all the crap it doesn't need. Meditation is the defecation of the soul.

Filmmakers should begin their day with zazen. Don't be eager to rush out and shoot something. Sit a while first. Maybe you'll take time to think things through. Maybe you'll think of something better. Maybe you'll think the whole thing over and think better of it. Maybe you won't think of anything. That's all right too. Maybe the best films are those that don't get made. Not making a film is a very important part of filmmaking.

Or, to paraphrase a famous Zen poem:
Sitting quietly doing nothing
and the film grows by itself.

Zen is a way of letting things happen. And letting them be. Zen is the moment in the moment aware of the moment. And cinema is the greatest collection of moments man has ever collected.
I sit at the moon-filled window
Watching the mountains with my ears.
Hearing the stream with open eyes . . .
The most fleeting thought is timeless,
A single hair's enough to stir the sea.

—Shutaku, 14th century

Zen is another word for Zest. For zip and zap and zing. If you have no appetite for life as it is, and are not excited by the koan of life's enigmas, then Zen is not for you. Try the Baptists instead. Zen has zest for the whole business from Z to A.

Zen really begins with A. And the words of A: *Alive. Awake. Alert. Aware. Agile. Adept.* Thus, to begin your own Zen, are you alive or are you just going through the motions?

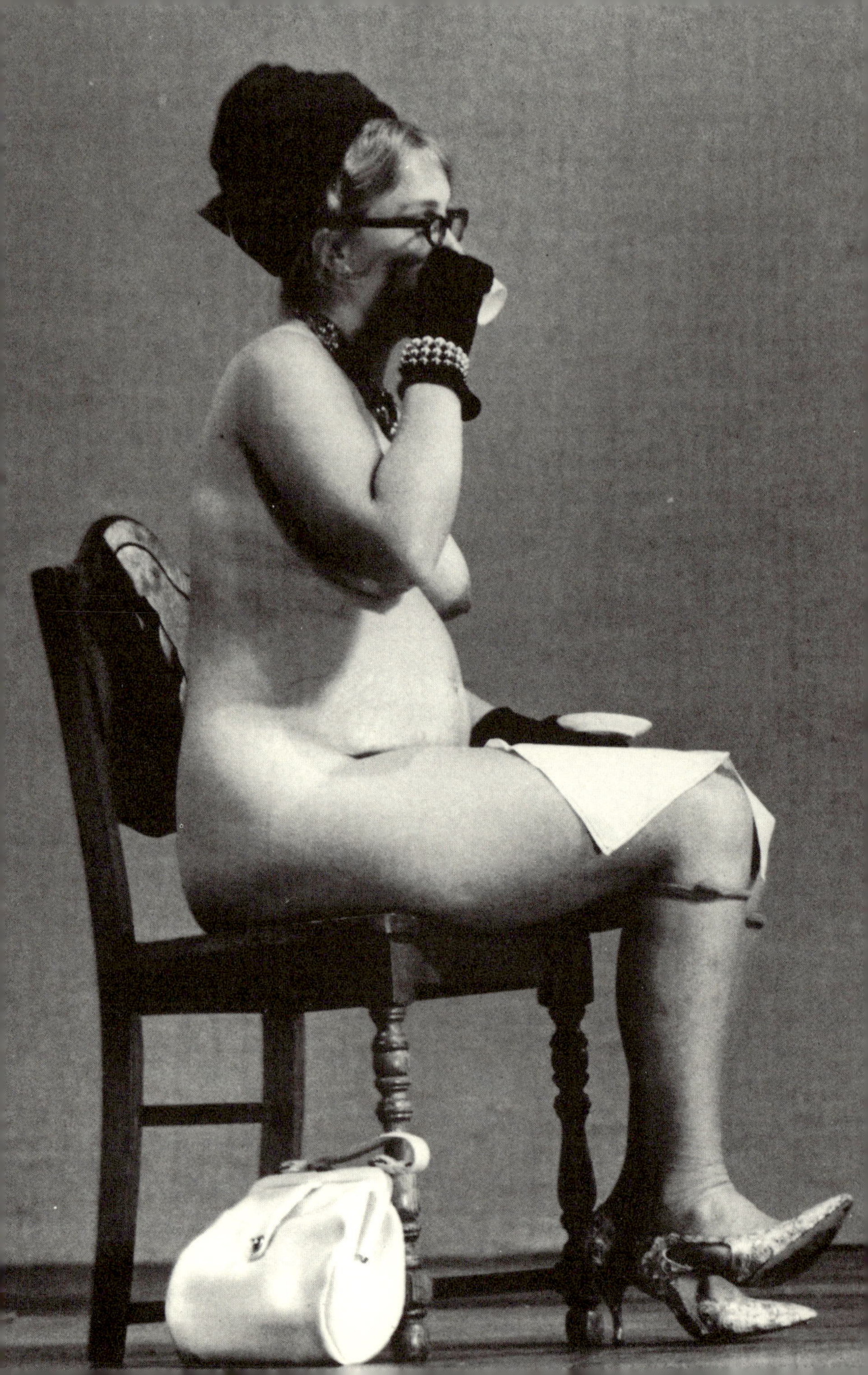

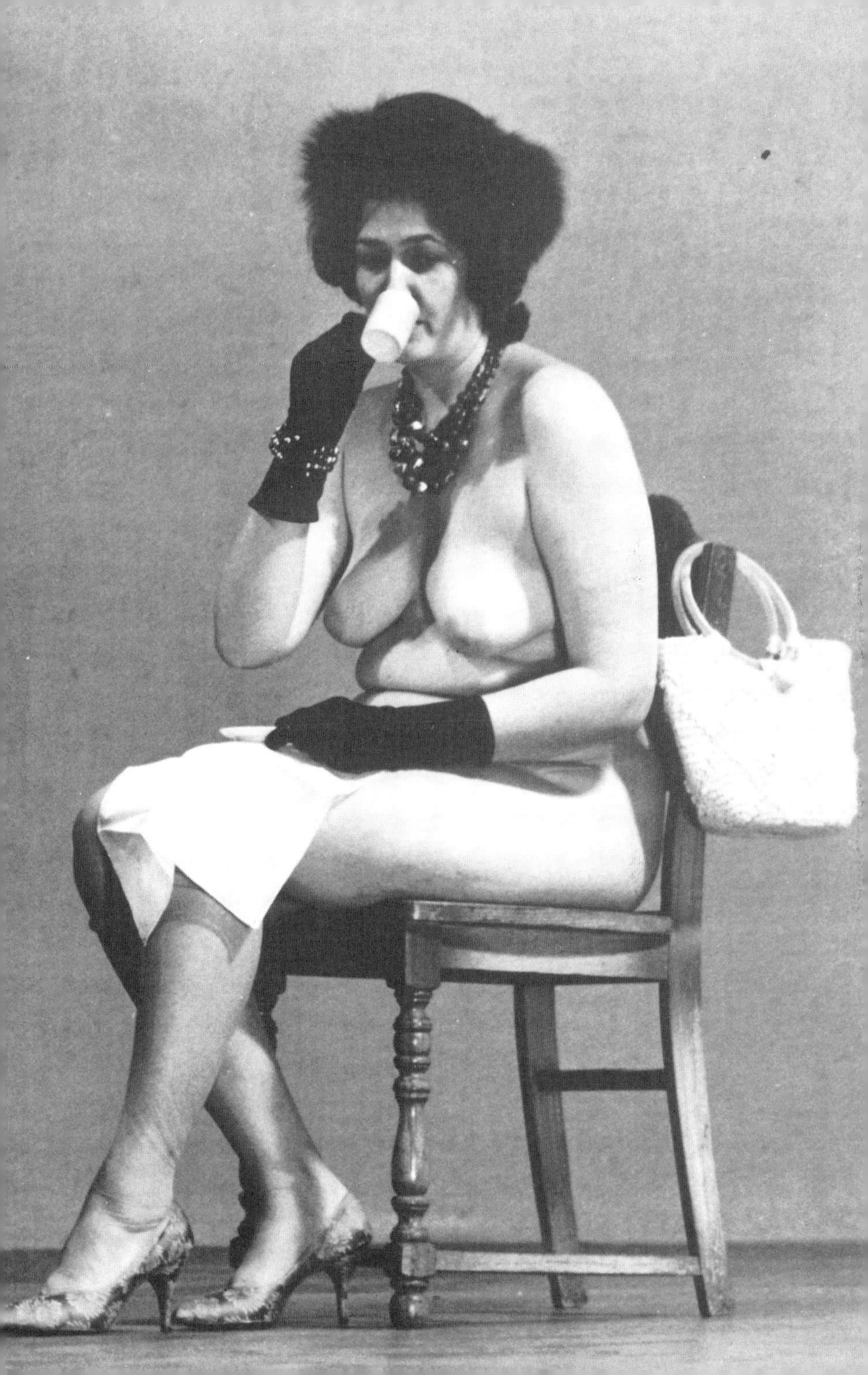

According to Mr. Takashi Ikemoto of Yamaguchi City, Zen poetry is characterized by conciseness, rigor, spontaneity, virility, and serenity.

The only films worth looking at more than once are those with Zen in them. Even a little Zen helps any movie.

Fritz Lang has no Zen. Busby Berkeley does. Vigo radiates it. Dovzhenko has it in his bones. Japanese films have too little Zen in them and too much John Ford. Buster Keaton is pure Zen. Visconti doesn't know what it is. Bergman has everything but. Woody Allen has nothing but.

Zen is a great nonsense word. Zen is often zany but it is completely serious. Zen has no patience with the worthy, the exhaustive, the grand.

Zen is a way of perceiving the serious nonsense of the universe. Hence it is the practice of true poets.

Mozart bubbles with Zen, Wagner hasn't a trace. Zen giggles with what is most profound. It knows that the irrational is the lifeblood of art. Mack Sennett has Zen without knowing it. Fellini has Italian Zen.

Above all, Zen has no respect for scriptures, for texts and theories, for the confusing inadequacies of language. Zen points directly at the thing itself.

When the Zen master pointed at the moon, he said, "Why are you looking at my finger?"

Zen is an art of seeing. It does not follow a script. It is not founded on written words but on direct experience. It is outside the established teachings. Hence Zen is truly avant-garde cinema.

Zen has nothing to do with bright ideas. It looks for the transcendental in the commonplace. Except that there is no commonplace. To the true poet nothing is trivial. "If he breathes into anything that was before thought small, it dilates with the grandeur and life of the universe," said Whitman, who breathed into grass.

Zen is poetry in action. It is the reality one creates out of what already exists. Its big movie is made out of innumerable haiku moments frame by frame. Zen is seeing the light in everything you see. It has nothing to do with preconceptions or goals. Joan Miro: "If you have any notion of where you are going, you will never get anywhere."

A Zen maxim says: "Don't smoke while peeing." More politely we could say: "Don't smoke while looking through the lens."

This is the moment to focus and center, this is meditation in action, this is the suchness of Is.
> This is It
> and I am It
> and You are It
> and so is That
> and He is It
> and she is It
> and It is It
> and That is That.

What you choose to make of It can come later. But first you have to realize where you are. The fish said to his mother: "I have heard a lot about the sea. Please tell me where it is."

Zen is not interested in comparisons, curriculums, concepts, careers. It wants living experience. Discussing Art is anti-Zen. "The poetic imagination," said Stephen Spender, "is harmed by absorbing more intellectual knowledge than it can digest."

Looking through your lens, are you in the Eternal Now? Couldn't you use a little Enlightenment?

Wake up. Wake others up. Be a Zen master. Hit the dumbbell over the head. With a slapstick. Or hit the slapper with a dumbbell. But awake!

There is nothing more surprising than right now. Right now is where you always are anyway.

Zen master Ikkyu was asked by a layman: "Master, will you please write for me some maxims of the highest wisdom?"

Ikkyu immediately took his brush and wrote the word "Attention."

"Is that all?" asked the man.

Ikkyu then wrote twice: "Attention. Attention."

"Well," remarked the man, "I don't see much in that."

Ikkyu then wrote three times: "Attention. Attention. Attention."

Irritably, the man demanded: "What does that word 'Attention' mean anyway?"

Gently, Ikkyu answered, "Attention means attention."

Whatever the price, pay attention. Pay attention whatever price it asks. Otherwise you will pay through the nose for your non-attention. "Craft is perfected attention," said Robert Kelly.

Do you practice zazen sitting on the naugahyde zafus in the movie theater? Or do you just sit there? Are you paying attention to what is happening or are you too busy forming an opinion? Are you seeing any Light?

A Japanese cabinet maker spent sixteen days preparing to make a simple cabinet. He then completed it in a few hours. When asked why he waited so long he said fifteen days were required to forget inessentials.

A blind man was offered a lantern when he was starting home at night.

"I don't need a lantern," he said, "light or dark is the same to me."

"But someone may run into you."

He took the lantern but had not gone very far when someone ran into him.

"Watch where you're going," said the blind man, "can't you see my lantern?"

"Your light is out, brother," came the answer.

Zen is anathema to critics because Buddhism insists that reality has nothing to do with good or bad, acceptance or rejection. From the Zen point of view questions asked by Western thinkers are either frivolous or impertinent. Huang Po said: "Only when you stop liking and disliking will all be clearly understood."

Validate your mind. If you don't have a point of view, how will you ever see the point? You are what you see. The world is the creation of your seeing. Live what you see. Live *in* what you see. Empty your mind of labels, ghouls, and goals!

Zen student: If I haven't anything in my mind, what shall I do?
Zen master: Throw it out.
Student: But if I haven't anything, how can I throw it out?
Master: Then carry it out.

Buñuel has Catholic Zen. Dreyer has Protestant Zen. Stravinsky has Russian Zen. Eisenstein almost lost his.

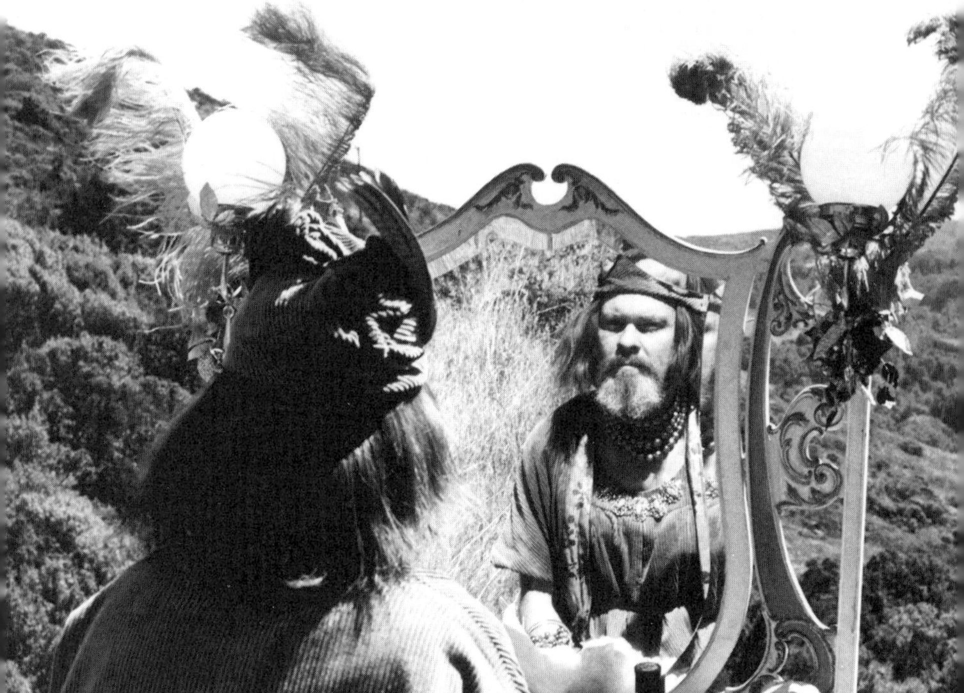

Precise spontaneity is the only way of hitting the target. When you know how to be where you are and to do what you have to do, you are ready for any risk. Order does not interfere with freedom, as Bach proved. Bach makes all kinds of freedom live together harmoniously.

The Zen filmmaker: Tranquil as a mountain, alert as a cat, natural as a hawk, spontaneous as a monkey, flowing like a river.

In his essay *Zen in European Art*, R. H. Blyth lists six qualities which should be present in any picture for it to be truly Zen. These are : naturalness, humor, agedness, latency, sexuality, and joy. Blyth explicates these aspects thus:

Naturalness includes simplicity, spontaneity, and inner quietness.
Humor means paradox, unconventionality, and freedom.
Agedness involves ripeness, timelessness, inevitability.
Latency implies the essence, the unknowable, the potential.
Sexuality illustrates Thoreau's saying, "All nature is my bride." Joy celebrates the exhilaration of reality.

The aim of the Zen film student: to see into his own cinema nature and into the cinema nature of Nature. Then perhaps enlightenment may knock his socks off. When you see the light for sure, you can throw away your light meter.

Said the Zen student: "How does it happen? Now that I am enlightened I am just as miserable as before."

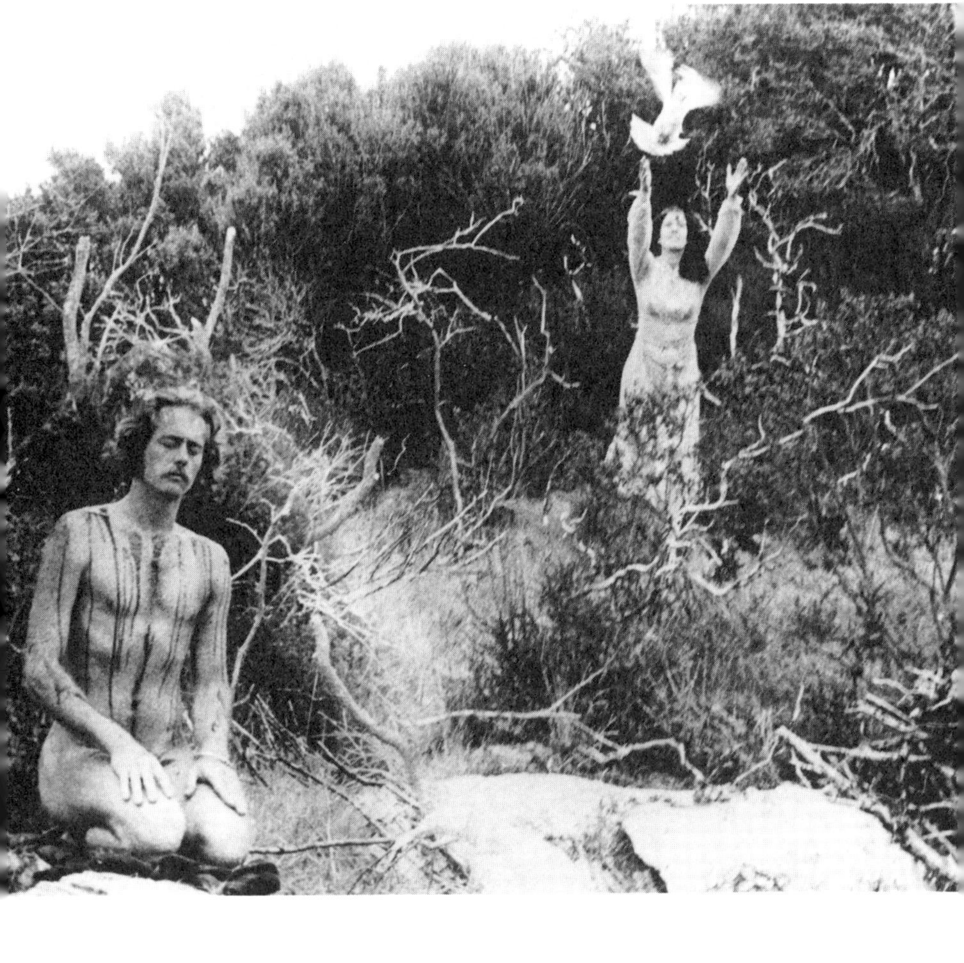

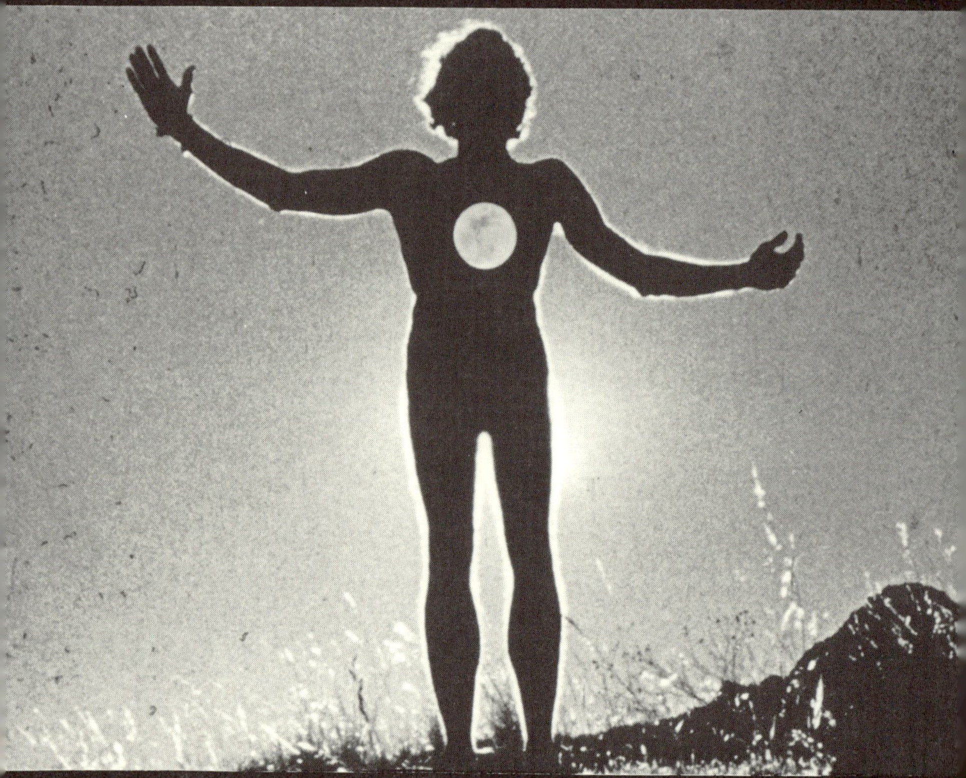

The Oz of Cinema

> It is a far, far better thing to
> have a firm anchor in nonsense than
> to put out on the troubled seas of
> thought.
>
> —J.K. Galbraith

Oz is a place poets should visit once a year. And before setting forth on any shooting party, filmmakers should stop off in Oz to remind them of what not to forget.

Oz is of a different order of nonsense from Zen. Zen is where you see what is.

Oz is where you see what isn't.

Oz is where there are no parents, no teachers, no preachers, no police, no experts, no press, and no need of any of them.

Oz is the land of the gleeful and the home of the daft.

Oz is the place to see the innocent Light in the heart.

Oz is an American Mother Goose Utopia. It is a fountain of youth. Or, more aptly, a fountain of childhood. Where Zen is the land of the zany sage, Oz is the land of the laughing boy. Zen is for the *senex*, Oz is for the *puer*. But they are not really far apart: the sage enjoys the wisdom of returning to his childhoodness.

Oz is run by witches and little girls. Its queen is a 10-year-old named Ozma. No one in Oz can get sick or grow old or die. No one earns a living, puts on weight, or thinks deeply. In short, Oz is everything the United States would secretly like to be.

The surest way of getting there: go to the heart of America. That would be Kansas. There get yourself into the cockpit of a cyclone. However, landing fields in Oz are unpredictable. Sensibly there is no airport near the capital. You are bound to come down in the middle of an adventure, not a predicament.

Like the cosmogony of the Navajos, Oz is a mandala composed of four equal countries, north south east and west, that have different colored landscapes. And at its center stands a most American "jewel in the lotus": a city made entirely of valuable green stuff, in this case emeralds.

Oz is where everyone is wealthy and no one is rich.

Oz is where you act foolish and end up wise.

Oz is where anything you imagine is likely to happen.

Oz is where the unexpected can always be counted on.

Oz is where you take down your pants anywhere.

Oz is where there is no advertising.

Oz is the playground where everything is done for love.

Oz is where there are no hucksters to interfere with your living moment.

Oz is where you never apologize, never explain.

Unless you have some Oz in you, you will go along with President Holdfast and General Apathy. You will believe in doctors, insurance companies, statistics, national defense, pensions, retirement communities, and a thoroughly safe dwindle. You will garner some fringe benefits but miss out on the central Benefit.

If you still have some Oz in you, you will grow younger as you age. You will not only have the serenity of seeing the Light, you will still trip lightly your own fantastic.

Chaplin and Cocteau have Oz in them. But Stroheim doesn't. Méliès had the most far-sighted. Judy Garland had the most successful.

Putting Oz in your film is arranging life to suit yourself. It is a way of prolonging and developing the games of childhood. It is a way of constructing more intricate toys. It is a way of being loyal to the playfulness of the spirit. It is a way of fooling around and accidentally discovering a new universe.

To the serious arbiters of taste any Oz is suspect: gaiety, fantasy, foolishness, and unremorseful sadness are plainly marks of a frivolous mind. So highbrows turn gratefully to works of murder, boredom and despair. And proclaim solemnities to be masterpieces because they are ponderous.

But in the free world of Oz a child can pluck honey from the paw of a bear.

The Oz of cinema is where you can keep your Divine Child uncontaminated by the ignorance of the educated. You can keep his wonder fresh, his irrationality pure, his feeling natural, his invention authentic, his laughter honest. In other words, ready to enter the Kingdom of Heaven.

In my own filmography Loony Tom has a certain Oziness. As do Game Little Gladys, the Gardener's Son, Princess Printemps, and the Aging Balletomane. The adults in *Mother's Day* are looking for a lost Oz. Mary Albion, the fat fairy godmother, came either directly from Oz or is on her way there; indeed *The Pleasure Garden* is a British annex of Oz. All of *The Bed* takes place in Oz.

Film nuts grow on trees in Oz. And all the cameras are magic kits. Ozians relish the unlikely, like true poets. It wouldn't hurt any filmmaker to take a few seminars with the Wizard of Oz and learn a little Hocus Focus. He himself learned a lot from that greatest of wizards, Georges Méliès.

Get some sleight into your hand. Learn the precision of the magician. Prestidigitation is a precious art that can go all the way from the rabbit in the hat to the manifestation of a god. With proper abracadabra momentous transformations can take place.

Some of the people who are at home in Oz: Candide, Klee, Edward Lear, Satie, Tolkien, Robin Hood, Shakespeare, Edith Sitwell, Miro, George McDonald, John Cage, Aleister Crowley, Lewis Carroll, Rousseau, Christian Morgenstern, Ronald Firbank, Edward Hicks, and Anonymous.

In recent years some particularly movie characters have moved into Oz. One of them is a dowager from the early days, Queen Trixie of Flix, who dwells in the Hall of the Great Silents. She has gotten fat from long sitting, her eyesight is defective, and she no longer knows one movie from another. But her magic movieola is always going and she loves everything she sees.

One of the muses of cinema sometimes visits queen Trixie of Flix: a shadowy alluring creature, who has a habit of fading out when you need her most. Her name is Oblivia. She makes filmmakers oblivious of everything but film and then leads them and their works into oblivion.

Some of the other muses of cinema are: Lumena, Opia, Ephemera, Insomnia, Nostalgia, and Synchronicita.

Above all of these is, of course, the great goddess CineMa, whom the residents of Cineoz worship religiously. She is a goddess of Time continually weaving for us and through us the fabric of her illusions of the world. All the movies which we imagine we experience in time are generated for us by her dancing web. Endlessly proliferating, she is our mother, our magic and our despair.

Long live the land of Oz, whatever name you give it, wherever you find it!

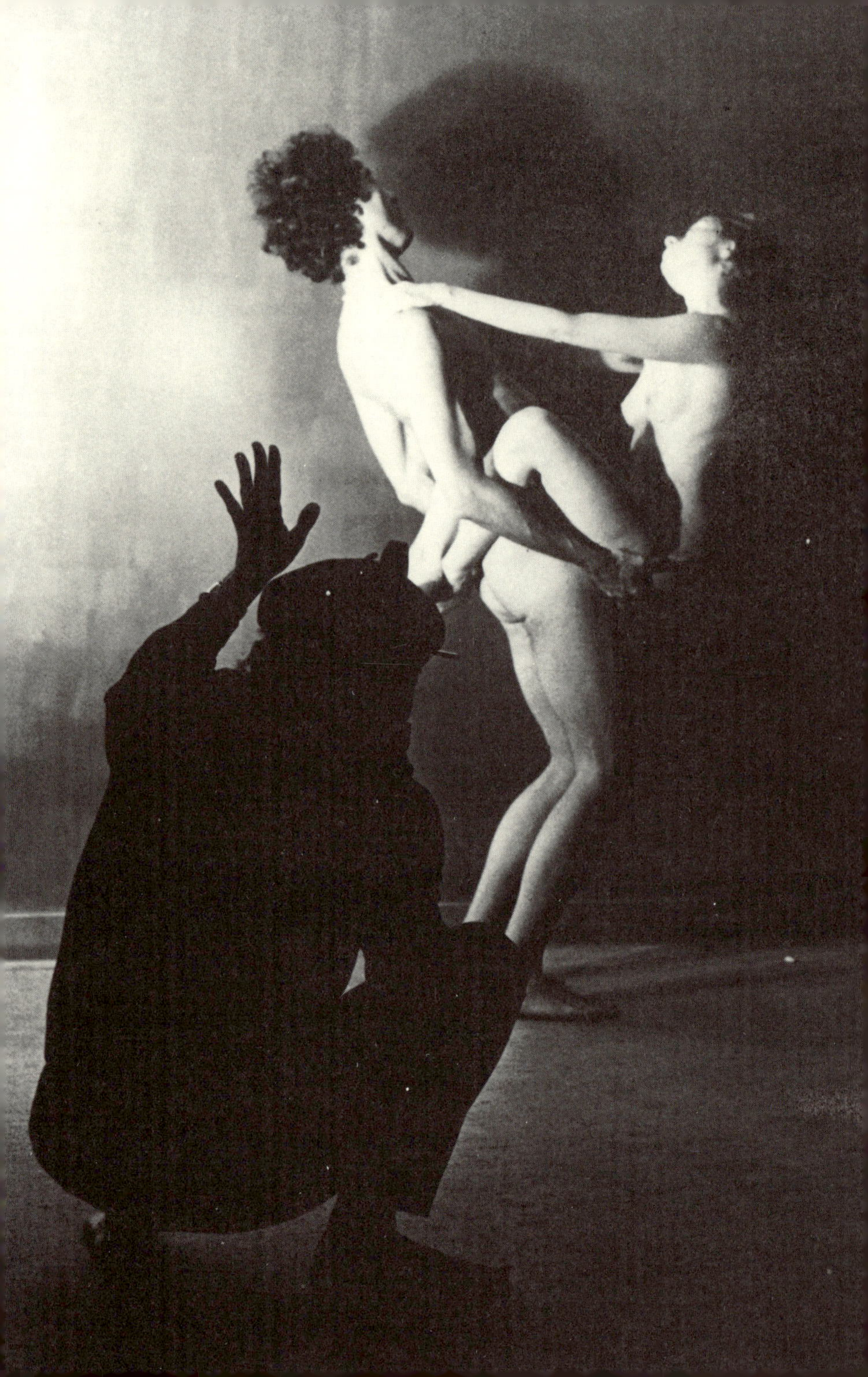

SOME DEFINITIONS

Kodakery: Pictures are more important than life.

Example: "Congratulations, madam. That's a fine looking child you have there."

"Oh, that's nothing. You should see his picture."

Movieology: Movies are more important than life.

Example: Among the large crowd not one person was looking at the eclipse of the moon. They were all standing in line at the box office.

Theorology: Theories are more important than movies and life.

Example: "When I am showing you a picture," said the professor, "it is more important for you to see what I say."

The Alchemy of Cinema

> I like a film to have a beginning,
> a middle and an end, but not
> necessarily in that order.
>
> —Jean-Luc Godard

Film has its own peculiar alchemy. This is inaptly called Editing. In truth it is the real opus of cinema.

In the editing chamber occurs the most crucial and often the most creative part of making a film: it partakes of the alchemical mystery.

Alchemy is the ancient art of transforming the raw matter of nature into a valuable essence. Sometimes, though rarely, this emerges as precious gold. Usually the alchemist is lucky if he gets quicksilver. That is an appropriate enough element for the silver screen.

Anyone (more or less) can shoot footage, as anyone (more or less) can put down words on a page. But what makes a film dance is the way the shots are put together.

Montage is an art of prestidigitation. How many possible layouts of the cards? How many rabbits in the hat? Throw all the shots into the air. See if they will fly. See where they will land. See if they will land at all. The cutting room: home of style. The editing board: arbiter of form.

Walt Whitman reassures us: "All truths lie waiting in all things." The alchemical adept puts his raw material through many changes to rid it of "impurities." What he seeks is solid substance of ineffable value, something "indescribable and inimitable" — which is how Renoir described the mystery of a great painting.

What can scissors and glue do? Let us juggle and join and juxtapose! O what scissors and glue can do!

In the dark of his laboratory the cinematic alchemist works for hours, days, months, years, seeking the seemingly impossible goal of metamorphosis. With his paraphernalia he tries to transform the invisible into the visible, or as Redon said, to "put the logic of the visible at the service of the invisible."

He searches for that continuously flowing Light which will transform leaden fragments into a single glowing jewel. Often enough, alas, his "original chaos" remains unredeemed.

Of the editing process Cocteau said: "To reorganize chance. That is the basis of our work." Chaplin told Cocteau that after making a film he "shakes the tree." One must only keep, he added, what sticks to the branches.

Editing is what you leave out: what you leave in has to be absolutely needed.

Alchemy is the art of Hermes, the great shape-changer. In the editing laboratory Hermes turns the film into the shape of an authentic illusion. The Humanist Patrizi proposed to Pope Gregory XIV: "Let Hermes take the place of Aristotle!"

In the very beginning, with *The Potted Psalm,* I learned that no two individuals edit the same footage in any similar way. Every man sees the world arranged to confirm his vision of it. From our joint footage Sidney Peterson extracted an emphasis quite different from my own version. Not only were two aesthetics and two mother complexes at variance; we were also two different kinds of alchemists. All alchemists might start from the same raw material, but each would end up with a unique philosopher's stone.

Alchemy reshapes what is not yet put together.

It unites with whatever incomprehensible wants to come into being.

It discovers a microcosm.

It releases the David hidden in Michelangelo's stone.

It unclothes the Inevitable.

"All things are beautiful if you have got them in the right order," said John Grierson.

With the putting together of *Mother's Day* I ventured deep into the alchemical mysteries of film. The completed footage hung for weeks in the bedroom of the Baker Street flat I shared with Kermit Sheets. Night after night the strips of film rustled in the breeze from the open window. I lay awake listening to them, wondering how they would ever fit together, waiting for them to tell me what sequence they preferred.

Eventually I sat at a dinky Craig viewer hour after hour learning the images, seeking their hidden correspondences, by trial and error gradually discovering an inevitable structure. This resembled deciphering the secret formula for an Open Sesame. I was more surprised than anyone by what emerged. And enormously grateful to the Guardian Deities who had made it happen. (They, I find, only like things that are allowed to grow into their true inevitability. They pay no mind to ready-mades.)

"Everything should be as simple as it is, but not simpler," said Albert Einstein.

The public is able to see only projected films, the poet of cinema has to see the unprojected ones.

I love going to the editing table. It is the altar of transformation mysteries. Dust it off devotedly. "Let us consecrate." At any moment a temporal ecstasy may occur.

Is this why professional film editors have the tranquility of priests whereas their missionary brothers out shooting wear a more worried look? Editing is a form of midwifery in which one has to be confident that a new creature will eventually be born.

78 Making Light of It

People who like puzzles make good editors. An emerging film is a diagramless crossword, a jigsaw without a known shape. Sometimes it resembles being lost in a dungeon. As Leonardo da Vinci put it, "You have to go up a tunnel backwards."

Wagner wrote of Beethoven: "All the pain of existence is shattered against the immense delight of playing with the power of shaping the incomprehensible."

Requirements of the alchemist: passion, perseverance and prayer. Some of the greatest raptures of cinema occur at the editing bench when an unexpected felicity emerges that is so appropriate and ineffable that one knows one has unraveled a truth. This is the Eureka moment: the flower has appeared in the stone. A finished film is composed of many such felicities, but they become so absorbed into the structure of the total work that they are taken for granted by the spectator as mere building blocks.

Blake: "It takes all of creation to make a single flower."

Practically speaking cinema is: putting images together in various musical measures. Editing is the music of cinema, as music is the architecture of time. Editing gives film its form, notation, counterpoint, development, pace, syncopation, and style. Such an alchemy should be spared the censorious term of Editing. The art is that of Composing. To edit film is to compose eye music. When you edit your work do you know what key you are in, what your signature is, what your measures are?

In order to qualify as alchemical adepts, novices in the Brotherhood of Light should be required to study music. This will help you to observe your images running through the viewer as musical notation rather than as a mere succession of scenes. This will reveal the form of your measures, your long and short notes, your rests, your intervals, your tempos. You will discover how much the composition of a film relies on its metrics. Thus you can better enjoy what goes on in, for instance, *A Movie* (Conner), *Arnulf Rainer* (Kubelka), *Dog Star Man* (Brakhage), and *Breathing* (Breer). If you ain't got rhythm, you'll never make it.

Vertov: "The essence of film is in the interval." In music the interval is the fixed relation between two notes. In cinema the interval occurs between two shots. This creates immediate motion. Editing can create many kinds of motion between shots. Have you digested Vertov, not to mention Eisenstein?

Learn from the best, learn from the masters. If you are a swan, don't hang around ducks. When he went to study modern composition under Schoenberg, John Cage was surprised that the pieces studied were Mozart sonatas.

In music any theme can be given whatever tempo and key you like. Similarly you can cut your filmed scene fast or slow; the image will convey its action either way. First, if you like, edit what the pictures are doing. Then recompose the whole thing metrically.

Cinema is a form of opera. Learn your notes. Count your frames. Articulate your rhythms. Phrase your line. Shape your tone. Measure your rests. Practice harmonics.

All art is a matter of timing, but none more so than this one. In film you can alter time in all directions. But every moment must count. Death to the inessential!

Furthermore in this medium of durations don't neglect to measure the timeless as well. Great alchemy moves with the primordial rhythms of The Only Dance There Is.

Is cinema a Byzantine art?

Putting a film together resembles most of all the art of mosaic. In your hand these myriad "tiles" of image, all the same size and shape, have to be trimmed, arranged, carefully placed, and glued together to make a total picture. But unlike *The Wedding of Theodora* a film mosaic is never seen in toto. Film is a mosaic on a spool which reveals its total luminosity only after it has been unreeled through Light. It is a mosaic in duration, many pointillist fragments in succession, totally present only when it has disappeared into darkness at The End. Like a symphony.

Hence in composing film we have a craft that might be called *Musaics*.

Broughton's Musaic Law: Thou shalt glue thy vision note by note until it dance the Light.

Some Mottos for Editing Room Walls

> Compose yourself. Then compose.
> Every frame is a moment of Now.
> Take nothing for granted.
> By all means try all means.
> When in doubt, cut.
> Attain the inevitable.
> Allness is ripe.

Some Useful Final Tests

1) Look at your film upside down. This not only gets some blood into your head, it will show you how well your work hangs together. You might discover that it is really one for the bats.

2) Look at your film with your back. With a mirror, watch your film projected over your left shoulder. This will not only show you what a mirror sees, it will test the sturdiness of your compositions.

3) Look at your film sideways (lying down is the easiest way). Do left and right work as well as up and down?

4) Look at your entire film in reverse. Does Effect stream solidly from Cause? Do Alpha and Omega have good connections? Does the musaic hold together backwards?

A film is never finished, it is only abandoned. But if we are wise we are not expecting perfection anyway, since nothing in life is perfect, art included. All we alchemists can hope for: to arrive somewhere close to our original vision. Or, at some more astonishing place than we imagined.

Thomas Aquinas said, "Perfection of thing is threefold; first, according to the constitution of its own being; secondly, in respect of any accidents being added as necessary for its perfect operation; thirdly, perfection consists in the attaining to something else as the end."

The value of pursuing any art is to live life more ineffably. Or, as Spengler put it, "We can understand the world only by transcending it."

My life has prospered when I have remembered to pursue the Essential, the Eternal, and the Ecstatic.

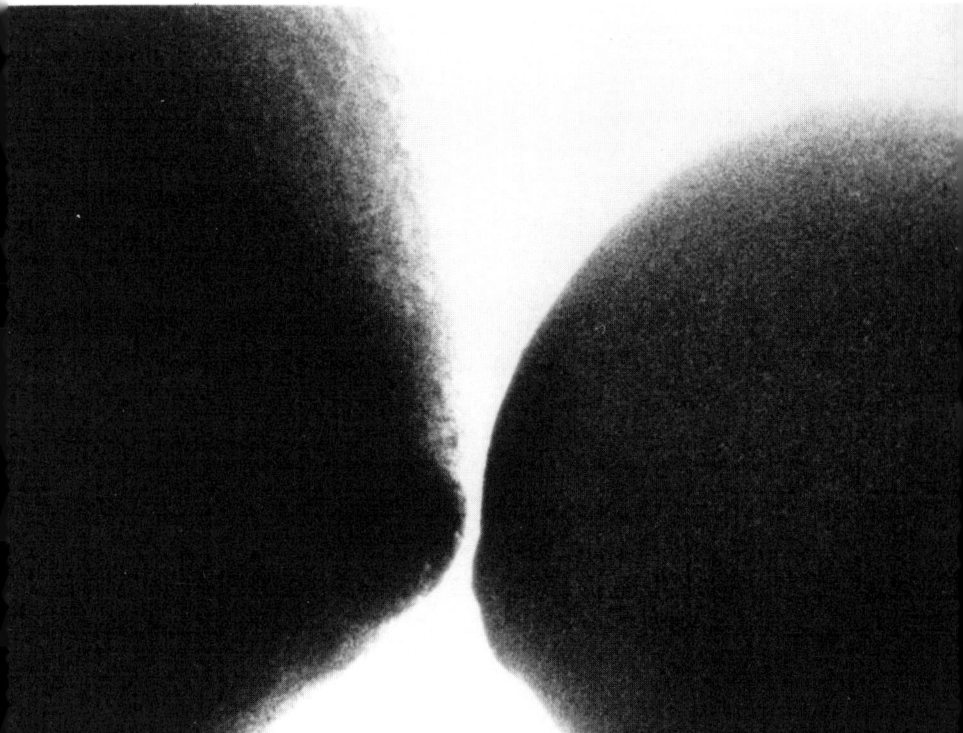

Some Fruits of Experience

Cinema is a public forum for private lunacy.

Cinema is a lie which makes us realize a truth.

An image of truth is whatever you believe in.

Without images the soul lacks wonder.

Without wonder there is no joy, without joy there is no magic, without magic there is no glory.

Film is both a mirror and an ever-expanding eye.

The eye sees more than the mind can know. The body knows more than either of them.

Movie images are dim reflections of the beauty and ferocity in mankind.

86 Making Light of It

The more original we are, the fewer we communicate with.

Genius is not having enough talent to do it the way it was done before.

If we fail to reach our glorious goals we can still bring back snapshots of the quest.

Keep going, even if you aren't going anywhere.

Cinema and the Tao

> The ocean takes care of each wave
> till it gets to shore.
>
> —Rumi

Inevitably the time comes to let your film go. This is the moment of last minute doubt. This is also the moment of Tao. And what does this old Chinese word have to do with filmmaking?

Tao is the opposite end of childhood Oz.

Tao is the pleasure garden of the old wise one.

Tao is the realization that one's effortful works are merely clouds in the wind.

Tao is how you finally surrender your creative anxieties.

Tao is the entire river of cinema flowing down into the murky sea of memory.

Tao is the alternating current that unreels the ever-changing, never-ending movie of practically everything.

Cinema includes its own Book of Changes. It has, in the end, little to do with works of art as such. It is not an infinite number of separate "things." It is a "sensitive chaos" in duration like the Tao itself. How can you consider something a public monument when, while you are looking at it, it is already floating down the river into Elsewhere?

If you will allow that your own work is part of the river of time, then it can become an amusement to watch whether it swims or sinks. Besides, you have already outgrown it. The picture you just took of what is happening is not what is happening now.

Tao is even harder to define than Zen. Tao is another nonsense syllable which the Chinese use as a name for the way everything grows, moves, changes, and interacts in its natural spontaneous order.

Zen sees that everything is what it is. Tao moves with everything as it flows.

Zen is the moment of awareness. Tao is letting the moment go.

The Tao of cinema affirms unbroken movement: it never stops, it never turns back, its patterns are real only as they pass. And every observer is himself part of this weblike river. This forms the never-ceasing cinema of our light and dark, great and small, dim and bright Yang and Yin.

The Secret of the Golden Flower, that mysterious text of Chinese alchemy, says that the Tao "cannot be seen. It is contained in the Light of Heaven. The Light of Heaven cannot be seen. It is contained in the two eyes." And in the space between the two eyes there sits a clairvoyant lens whereby the Light of Heaven circulates.

If you accept the principal of Eternal Change as governing the universe, then to work in a perishable medium like film means that you accept the universe. Yield and go with it, in the same way that a film flows through camera and projector, clicking, bending, warping, scratching, ripping, flickering, burning, shining. Yield, and toss your movie into the great river.

What does it matter that you don't know where your films go, who sees them or who doesn't? Either you trust a river, or you don't. Tao means knowing that you don't know, and being happy about it.

Certainly you are free to struggle upstream as much as you want to. You can dam your waters. Or divert them to various forms of husbandry. Or drain your swamp and dwell in a desert. But in the end all matters erode, melt, wash away, return to their source. This I tried to express in my film for Lao-tzu, *The Water Circle*, by flowing with a song of renewal and showing the waters as a hand-held dance of Light.

Once I dreamed of the Tao as a fine roomy boat which all Brothers of Light secretly knew about. And when the time came they would all climb aboard and rock merrily upon the currents as they floated down the filmy river of timelessness.

As Heraclitus might have said, the cinema you stand in is not the cinema you stepped into.

A Taoist is a man whose knowledge and intuition teach him how to harmonize with "unexpected turbulence" even when he lacks any seat belt to fasten. The ultimate tranquility beyond time and change is the condition of the Taoist immortal. And in their orchid heaven these Immortals drink plum wine, not bitter tea.

Ezra Pound said: "What thou lovest best remains, the rest is dross."

In Taoist cinema there is no black and white dualism. Its dark is always into its light and its light is always into its dark, for these are not absolutes. They continually flow into one another, overlap, become their opposites. This is symbolized on the revolving wheel of the Tai Chi, at the beginning and ending of *Nuptiae*. That symbol suggests the eternal movie of the Relative Absolute (or Absolute Relative) which might well be expressed by a transcendental double exposure.

Does there exist any true Taoist film which uses double exposure metaphysically to reveal the play of opposites in every moment of our being?

Buddhistically speaking, cinema is just a way of filling the Void. Or, trying to. Will the Void ever get completely filled with movies? If so, will it overflow with old cinematic defecations?

Ask yourself: why do you want to add to this shitpile?

Rilke insisted, "A work of art is good if it has grown out of necessity." Most art works seem to have an instinctive affinity for the nonessential. Stravinsky's customary response at concerts of earnest new music: "Who needs it?"

To be a good revolutionary, the way Stravinsky was, you need also to be a proper conservative. Cherish everything that nourishes the spirit, conserve the sources and resources of the past which can be renewed, and so create rebirths.

Lou Harrison has this alliterative motto: "Cherish, conserve, consider, create."

Baldinucci wrote of Bernini: "Preternaturally strong until his last illness, Bernini worked at his sculpture tirelessly, sometimes for seven hours at a time, and always with someone at hand to prevent him from falling off the scaffolding. He worked as if in a trance, and when an assistant urged him to stop and rest, his reply was: 'Leave me alone. I am in love.' "

Love is the ultimate Light. And the Tao is the dance of that Light. Why not devote your life to being so in love? Can you think of a more absorbing way to use your time?

Why not take what Keats called The Risk of Happiness? Why do you think you have a third eye?

Shift your tripod, change your focus: you might see the Light. You might even see the Glory of God. Then you could be eligible for such an ineffable compliment as the one that a lady paid to the sculpture of David Tolerton: "Is it real," she asked, "or did you make it?"

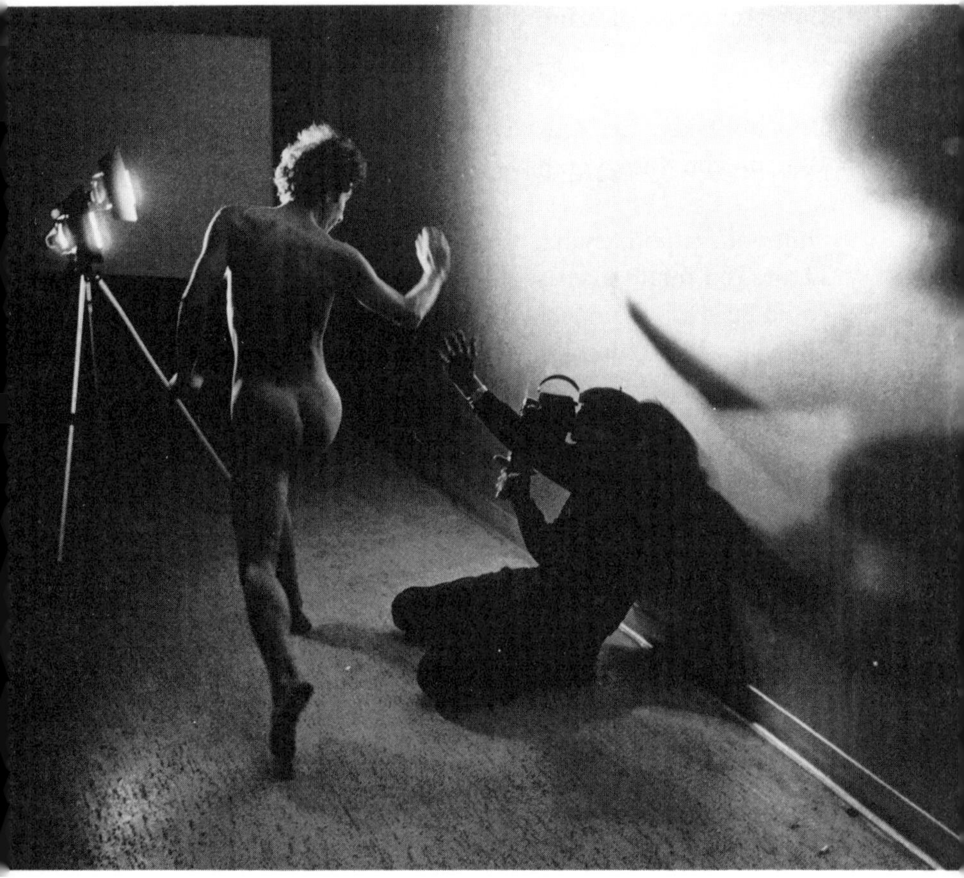

Making Lights of My Own

> I love Mickey Mouse more than any woman I've ever known.
>
> —Walt Disney

All of my films have been love affairs of the art. From *The Potted Psalm* in 1946 to *Scattered Remains* in 1988 I could not have created anything without sharing love with my collaborators.

Cinema lit up my life when I discovered at age thirty-two a wondrous reality: the love that flows between fellow artists. And the more intense the love, the livelier the work. Eros is a true source of the light. "Relations are real, not substances," said Buddha.

My films have been made with love and for love, made with the love of others and for those I loved. And for the most part they all celebrate irrepressible instinct and erotic triumph. John Lilly said, "Like it or not, cosmic love is absolutely ruthless and highly indifferent." This is what wags the world. Things only work when the relentless current of love is plugged in.

I have called my fellow workers in the medium a Brotherhood of Light and this Brotherhood is for me where ardors and imaginations are partnered. There can be no seeing of the light unless there is love to ignite it.

Fortune blessed me with gifted and sympathetic brothers of this light. In the shared adventures of my twenty-two films all the helping hands, performers, cameramen, composers were remunerated mainly with praise and picnic lunch. But since mixing-studios and printing laboratories don't believe in love they plunged me into debt.

Following my initiation by Peterson with *The Potted Psalm* I began my first personal film, *Mother's Day*. This and three subsequent works were made in San Francisco between 1947 and 1951 with the lovelight collaboration of Frank Stauffacher and Kermit Sheets. In London in 1952 I began location work on *The Pleasure Garden*. These five black and white films, made outdoors in natural settings, sum up my early preoccupation with life as a playground for the aches and ardors of love.

MOTHER'S DAY (1948) 23 minutes

What became *Mother's Day* began as scenes for a film version of my play *The Playground*. But I found myself wanting to reexamine indelible memories from my San Francisco childhood. Inevitably the dominant figure of the mother entered the field of play as an indifferent goddess disapproving of romp and spoof. "Mother was the loveliest woman in the world and Mother wanted everything to be lovely." But behind her back the children (acted by adults) live out their secrets and fantasies, eventually escaping the thrall of propriety.

Mother's version of events went like this: "Once upon a time there was a very beautiful and refined young girl who had a great many suitors. But she married the wrong one. Then she had a great many children and she did not know what to do with them either."

ADVENTURES OF JIMMY (1950) 11 minutes

A lonely innocent from the backwoods goes to the Big City searching for an ideal mate. He is stalked by ladies of the town, lodges in the slums, exhausts himself in a dance hall, tries prayer and poetry and psychoanalysis. Thanks to his naive persistence, his quest proves alarmingly successful.

This parody of a stereotypical fable I made as a spoof of my own idealism. I enacted the title role to mock my awkward pursuit of love objects.

FOUR IN THE AFTERNOON (1951) 15 minutes

This was my first film using poems for a shooting script, each movement a variation on the reveries of desire.

Game Little Gladys with her jumprope envisions possible love mates:
>Ten is the number
>of the husbands in my heart
>Which one will count me
>his true sweetheart?

The Gardener's Son imagines nymphs and Venuses dancing in his park:
>Pure will blow my love,
>honeyed will she be:
>O what beautifying of the bee!

Princess Printemps is chased around a ruined palace by a love-crazed courtier:
>Spring
>   Spring
>   runs around a green riddle
>   hey diddle
>   hooray!

The Aging Balletomane conjures in his backyard the lost ballerina of his dreams:

> O ago so long, how it passed!

LOONY TOM, THE HAPPY LOVER (1951) 11 minutes

The poem that inspired this picture begins:

> Give me a tune and I'll slap the bull fife,
> I'll spring the hornblower out of his wife.
>
> Any old flutist you care to uncover,
> Give me his name and I'll be her lover.
>
> > La diddle la, the hydrant chatted.
> > Um titty um, the milkpail said.

Enacting Tom as a blissful baggy-panted Pan, Kermit Sheets cuddles a country wife, chases a bevy of milkmaids, lays a stern widow on the floor, and goes blithely singing on his way, all in the style of silent slapstick comedy.

THE PLEASURE GARDEN (1953) 38 minutes

After its showing at the Edinburgh Film Festival in 1951 several admirers of *Loony Tom* formed a committee to raise money for me to make a film in England. They included Basil Wright, Gavin Lambert, and Denis Forman of the British Film Institute. With Lindsay

Anderson as producer, I developed a comic fairy tale in the style of British "pantomime." A fat fairy godmother routs a puritanical Minister of Public Behavior and bestows love unions on the daydreaming strangers in a public park, with everyone singing at the end:

> Love is a pleasure, please.
> It's twice the pleasure
> to come together
> and make a pleasure for two.

Filmed in the ruins of the Crystal Palace Gardens, this celebration of love included a large company of professional actors and a 35mm cameraman, Walter Lassally. To my astonishment it gained a special prize at the Cannes Festival in 1954.

After an interval of a dozen years writing and teaching I was prodded back into filmmaking by Jacques Ledoux of the Royal Belgian Cinematheque. In 1967 he sent me a box of 16mm color film, begging me to create something for his International Film competition in Knokke-le-zoute. During the "summer of love" in San Francisco I managed to complete *The Bed* in time for the December opening of his festival.

In the ensuing eight years, between 1968 and 1976, I released eight more films in color. They owe their existence to the many cohorts who make the Brotherhood of Light a joy to belong to. They are further indebted to the

Jerome Foundation, the Guggenheim Foundation, and the National Endowment for the Arts.

THE BED (1968) 20 minutes

I had long been obsessed by the importance of beds in human affairs, even having written a poem that began:
> Everything important in life
> occurs upon a bed.
> It's where you cry when you are born
> and where you lie when dead.

I wanted to use a bed as a stage for the variety acts of the human comedy. My theme: "All the world's a bed, and men and women merely dreamers."

I was fortunate to have a brash live wire for a cameraman. Bill Desloge also brought with him attractive young hippies to perform. I lured my older friends like Alan Watts and Imogen Cunningham to join in acting out my scenes of humanity in capering moments of desire.

Roger Somers' orchard on the mountain above Muir Woods became the Eden place where Jehovah could send down from Heaven a white wrought-iron bed for Adam and Eve to begin the dance of human history.

NUPTIAE (1969) 14 1/2 minutes

Since he was present as best man, Stan Brakhage had insisted that I let him film the three ceremonies of my wedding to Suzanna Hart in 1961: at the City Hall, at the altar, and privately at the seashore. This footage formed the basis for what I later developed into *Nuptiae*. This included much optical printing, plus music by Lou Harrison with a chorus singing an epithalamium.

THE GOLDEN POSITIONS (1970) 32 minutes

Naked human bodies in movement have always entranced me. In attempting a pseudo-documentary of undressed humanity I took inspiration from the pioneer studies of Edweard Muybridge, from Alan Watts telling me that Confucius considered standing, sitting, and lying the golden positions of life, and from the Catholic Mass as the form to parody for this celebration of the holiness of the physical body. I filmed a variety of naked persons in various tableaus of the three positions, including the creation of Adam, a swift history of art, religion and social behavior, with a finale of sublime erotic poses. For this last section a chorus sings a kyrie:

> Body, have beauty upon us.
> Spirit, have beauty upon us.
>   Your body be with you.
>   And with your spirit.

Adroitly photographed by Fred Padula's Beaulieu, this playful solemnity includes a farcical solo by dancer Anna Halprin.

THIS IS IT (1971) 10 minutes

Watching my two-year-old son occupy the eternal moments of childhood play, I tried to capture his wonder with a little parable of Eden in our own backyard. Papa God in a treetop and Mother Earth inside a red ball speak the teachings of the world. David Myers' camera followed Baby Adam from the garden out to the streets of Mill Valley, while the ball chants its mantra:

> This is It
> This is really It
> This is all there is
> and It's perfect as It is.
> There is nowhere to go but Here
> There is nothing Here but Now
> There is nothing now but This
> And This is It.

DREAMWOOD (1972) 46 minutes

> Somewhere there is a forest
> somewhere at the center of the world

> there is a forest of the dream,
> a sacred wood, a grove of initiation.
> Somewhere there is what there has always been:
> the treasure hard to attain,
> the lair of the Great Goddess,
> the bed of the ultimate rapture.

On an island in the Kingdom of Her there is a labyrinthine grove where the Goddess manifests in many forms to challenge any intruder. No one but an obsessed poet in pursuit of his muse would dare to penetrate this perilous realm of the feminine powers. To the hero who persists in his quest to win her favor and be reborn within her, the Great Mother will reveal her ultimate secret.

This homage to Cocteau flows from my own poet's blood and unfolds in the cadences of mythic ritual. In the summer of 1970 John Schofill brought his Arriflex from the Chicago Art Institute to make images of fierce clarity for my apparitional narrative. For the rites of initiation we created a sacred wood in Mount Tamalpais State Park, not without harassment from the rangers. Kermit assisted me throughout, Henry Taylor endured the poet's trials valiantly, and Morton Subotnik supplied the music.

HIGH KUKUS (1973) 3 minutes

An homage to Basho, particularly to his famous haiku of the jumping frog, this film stares for three minutes

Making Lights of My Own 105

into a pond at the Japanese Tea Garden in Golden Gate Park, observing the subtle changes that take place in a quiet fragment of time. Not being Japanese I created my own terse verse form, more anthropomorphic than Basho ever allowed. Alan Watts called it cuckoo haiku.

> I have no desire to move about,
> said the Tree,
> I'm very attached to my roots.
>
> I like where I'm sitting,
> said the Toad,
> What else is a toadstool for?
>
> I have no meaning,
> said the Film,
> I just unreel myself.

TESTAMENT (1974) 20 minutes

In 1972 I was invited to present a speech at the opening of the new county library in the town of Modesto, California. The librarian wanted an inaugural address by an author who had been born in the town. I was the only candidate they could unearth. When I explained to my class in Film Directing at San Francisco State University that I would be unable to meet them on the day of the event, they proposed staging a "homecoming" parade for me through the streets of the town. From the footage of that colorful occasion, I spun what I thought would be my final film: a self-portrait bouncing me from my babyhood to my imagined death. To summarize the quest for erotic transcendence that animated all my cinema I mixed film clips, still photos and staged scenes. I was assisted at the camera by an ingratiating redhead named H. Edgar Jenkins, who had filmed the Modesto parade in slow motion. At the film's beginning I am seen rocking in a chair by the Pacific Ocean, questioning my life:

> I asked the Sea how deep things are.
>
> O, said She, that depends upon
> how far you want to go.

THE WATER CIRCLE (1975) 3 minutes

Celebrating the circulation of the waters of the world this homage to my favorite sage Lao-tsu is illustrated by the dance of sunlight on the sea. My accompanying verse was composed to the music of a Gigue by Corelli from his Concerto Grosso No. 9 in A, performed on the harp by Joel Andrews.

> Down and up they go
> the waters that always flow
> the rivers that open their veins to the sea
> and then return as snow.
>
> Down from arterial hills
> their circulation spills
> the heart of the lake refills

and down in the valley the river will sing
    as it refreshes everything
        high or low
        fast or slow
        from head to toe
        scenery   machinery
and makes the poppy grow.
It wakens a sleeping tree
it sets the salmon free
       and then flows down
       and down
       through field and town
      to drown in a briny shroud
      and resurrect into a cloud.

EROGENY (1976) 8 minutes

After praising the human body as an object to observe in *The Golden Positions* I envisioned a companion piece: the body as a terrain to explore. The opportunity for this came through the Pittsburgh Film-makers, with the collaboration of Robert Gaylor on camera and Robert Haller in production. The major technical hurdle was finding persons in Pittsburgh willing to take off their clothes. Shooting took place in March of 1975 in Sally Dixon's dining room during a snowstorm.

The poem on the soundtrack, written to fit the images, begins:

>   Reach
>   Touch
>   Discover
>
> We are hemispheres
>   ebbing and flowing
> We are continents
>   meeting
>
> Discover
>   my oases
>   Explore me

Though I had assumed my film career was finished with *Testament*, one day a young Canadian named Joel Singer walked into my classroom at the San Francisco Art Institute. He had developed unusual techniques created entirely in his Beaulieu camera. We were basically cinematic opponents: where I relished slow motion effects Joel's passion was speedy single framing. Perhaps an attraction of opposites sparked the eight films we made together between 1976 and 1988. Our collaboration began in fun with *Together*.

TOGETHER (1976) 3 minutes

Joel proposed an experimental portrait of me using his special effects. In the finished product I was amazed to watch the two sides of my head slowly coming together in fluctuations of repulsion and attraction. For the soundtrack I wrote a verse which concludes:

> together
> > altogether wholly in toto in toto
> > in totally toto together altogether
>
> together

WINDOWMOBILE (1977) 8 minutes

This is a mobile-home movie, made when Joel and I had moved into "a yellow mobile home in an unlikely neighborhood" where we looked out of windows and looked at windows reflected in windows. Joel taught me how to transform ordinary scenes into extraordinary games. For the sound I practiced a Pachelbel sonata and wrote a verse, while outside blackbirds were at their choir practice for an audience of frogs.

> They were seeing the light there
> They were seeing the day and the night every
> > day there
> They were looking and they were seeing
> They were living there in the light at that time.

SONG OF THE GODBODY (1977) 11 minutes

Joel's next portrait of me was of my body. At first I objected that it was too ancient a subject. But Joel agreed with Lin Yutang that "beauty is what is old and mellow and well-smoked." With hand-held close-ups moving over my flesh Joel created a geographical landscape of unrecognizable prairies and bushes. This became the scenery for my long poem that gives voice to the life force which animates each of us and which I call The Godbody.

> I breathe you   I contain you   I propel you
> I am your opening and closing
> I am your rising and falling
> I am your thrust and surrender
>
> I stiffen you   I melt you   I energize
> I quicken your humor and heartache
> I set the spark to your fluid
> I stir your mixable blessing . . . &c

HERMES BIRD (1979) 10 minutes

Hermes is the god of poets, doctors and thieves. He is also messenger of the gods and of the godbody in the phallus. I wished to honor this chakra of creation which is every man's pride, embarrassment and joy.

> This is the secret that will not stay hidden
> this secret that is no secret
> Such power thrives against every denial
>
> Here is the wonder of the god in man
> Here is the dangling flower of Eros
> This is He who awaits his ecstasy

To watch the subtle pulsations of a penis growing erect I filmed in extreme slow motion. Access to one of the official cameras used to photograph the atomic bomb explosions in the South Pacific allowed me to capture the slowest ascension of a penis that has ever been seen.

THE GARDENER OF EDEN (1981) 8 1/2 minutes

In 1980 Joel and I lived on a rubber plantation on the island of Sri Lanka. This vernal paradise belonged to the tallest man on the island who was also its most famous horticulturist. I pictured him as God trying to keep an eye on the flowering proliferation of his world. This dance of nature sings of the lost Eden we all search for but do not expect to find. Joel's camera work is itself an ecstatic dance. The music was performed on twin conch shells.

> Every day I grow a dream in my garden
> where the beds are laid out for love
> When will you come to embrace it
> and join in the joy of the dance?

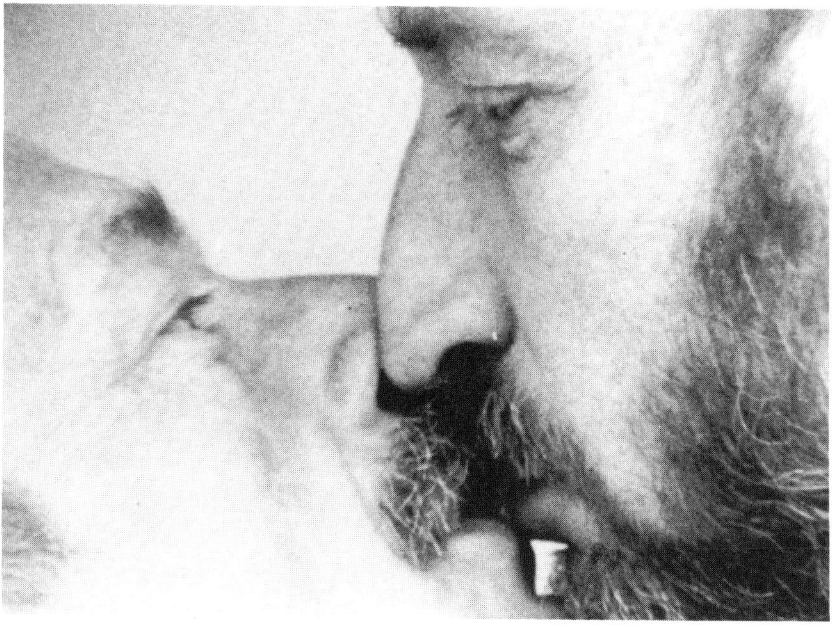

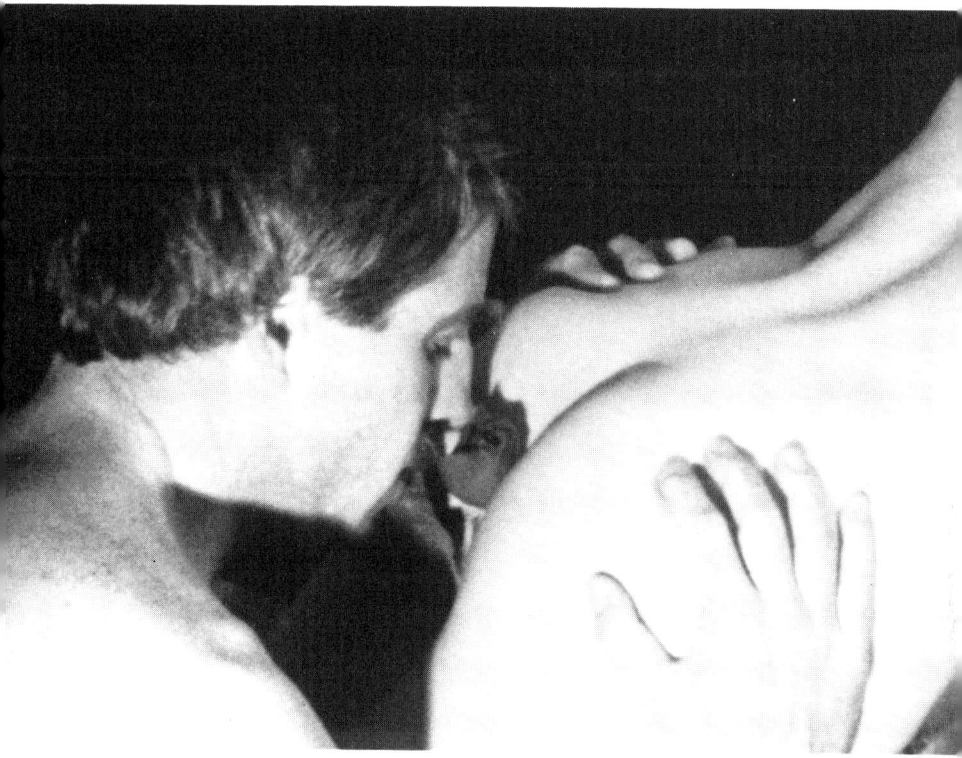

SHAMAN PSALM (1981) 8 minutes

Shocked by a century of ceaseless war-making, I wrote a poem pleading for a world of peace-loving comrades. When we attended a large men's gathering in Colorado Joel photographed random scenes of the group activity. These we later organized into a flow of images to accompany my reading of the antiwar canticle, which begins:

> Listen Brothers Listen
> The alarms are on fire
> The oracles are strangled
> Hear the pious vultures
> condemning your existence
> Hear the greedy warheads
> calling for your death
> Quick while there's time
> Take heed   Take heart
> Claim your innocence
> Proclaim your fellowship
> Reach to each other
> Connect one another
> And hold

DEVOTIONS (1983) 22 minutes

Men are the victims of a society that approves only of competitive conformists and insatiable consumers. I believe men are capable of happier pursuits. If a man keeps wonder in his eye, compassion in his heart, frolic in his balls, and abandon in his limbs he can dance hand in hand with his life and his death and reap a full harvest of love.

Joel and I set out to show some of the ways that men can enjoy one another without resorting to insult or aggression. We filmed forty-five couples in a variety of locations from Seattle to San Diego. In the brief overture Virgil Thompson is seen conducting the film's composer, Lou Harrison, playing the flute opposite his life partner William Colvig.

> Come forth brother souls
> claim your liberty
> Time for devotion
> time to fraternize
>
> Bring your orbits
> into harmony
> Time to plant starseed
> in one another's eyes

SCATTERED REMAINS (1988) 14 minutes

In 1988 when the San Francisco International Film Festival planned to honor me with a tribute to my forty years of filmmaking, I thought it apropos to prepare a new work for the occasion. Joel proposed making yet another portrait of me, this time his "Portrait of the Poet as James Broughton." He devised a dozen techniques to enliven my reading of a dozen poems. The last of these is, "I hear the happy sound of one hand clapping / all the way to Buddha land." In the final image clowns first seen on a beach at the beginning reappear transformed into Pan and Hermes dancing away toward the sea.

Looking For a Future

> O wad some Power the giftie gie us
> to see oursels as others see us!
>
> —Robert Burns

This poet's prayer was answered by the invention of the lens which gave us a new gift for self knowledge. Casting its eye upon human beings, it has produced widely conflicting reports. Focusing upon the spectacles of modern history in every corner of the world, it has gathered a voluminous and bewildering record of the 20th century. But what has the lens done for the souls of man? And what is the future of its capacity for vision?

Not only his art but man himself is still in the making. He continues to repeat his mistakes, to swing from approbation to condemnation, to cudgel his love objects, to worship conformity more than intelligence, to ignore the existence of poets and the insights of the wise. Can cinema in any of its manifestations encourage the maturing of the species?

To speculate on the future encourages the practice of hope. Might the cameras of the world provide transformative experiences? Increase the dissemination of amity and compassion? Nourish the risks of delight? Offer meditations, mantras and myths? Stimulate quest, daring and fulfillment? Might the lens help us to see ourselves as the "Others" see us, the angels for instance? What special presentation will goose the couch potato?

Video brings images of elsewhere into bed with us. What are viewers looking for in the thousands of images that have invaded the home life of the planet? Are they looking for anything, or are they looking to avoid everything? Could cinema be an instrument of redemption instead of a repository for triviality? Is it possible for the modern household to be more than an electronic receiving station for noisy distraction?

Certainly we need more than what James Hillman calls the "fast foods flung to the soul by our tyrants of the media." Have we lost the capacity to inhabit a fecund imagining? If we do not resharpen what has been dulled, how shall we fulfill our potential as creative beings? Could television possibly become the ultimate metaphysical guru?

If the forms of cinema could link the souls of the world into a loving global unity we might all see ourselves as one planetary phenomenon instead of a disparate globe of warring states. That would be closer to how the angels see us.

"Only he who keeps his eye fixed on the far horizon will find his right road," said Dag Hammarskjold.

What is our horizon? A worldwide Brotherhood of Light and Love may be a giant unlikelihood, but we can act as if it were going to happen, as if it were already secretly happening. We can act both *as if* and *in spite of.* In spite of the world's indifference, in spite of poverty, sickness and death, in spite of the word NO.

One must always do the impossible. Art itself is impossible. Trust the passion, the way of seeing, the zest of creating. There is no meaningful life without poetry and nothing is art that lacks it.

What unimagined radiance will yet emerge from the flickering dark?

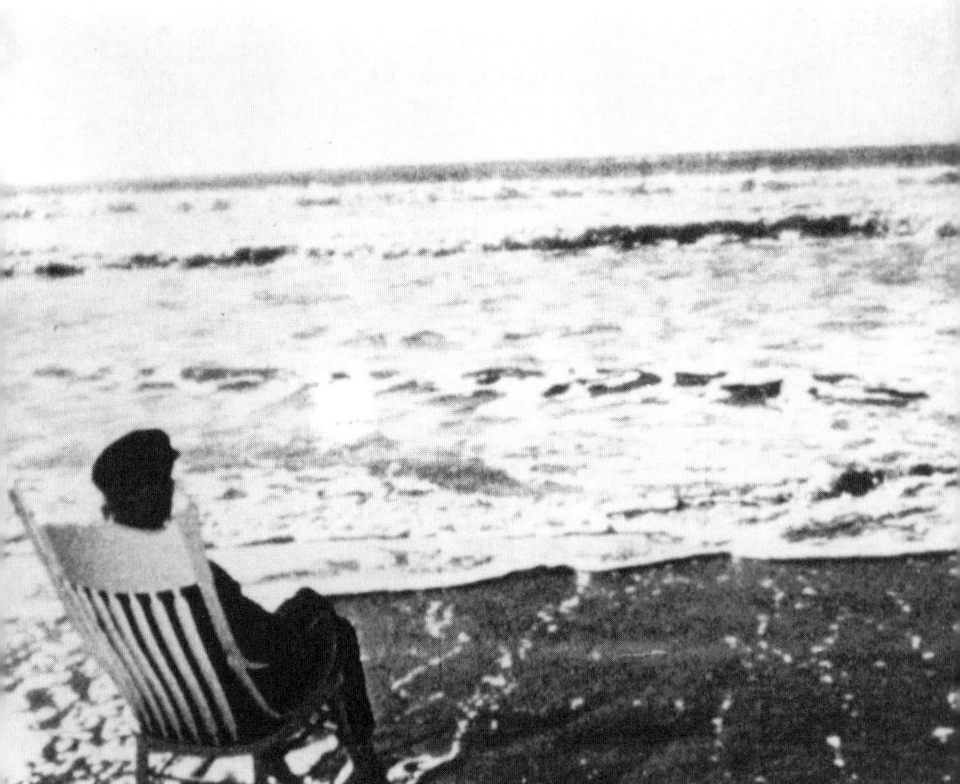

FILMOGRAPHY

1946	*The Potted Psalm*
1948	*Mother's Day*
1950	*Adventures of Jimmy*
1951	*Loony Tom*
1951	*Four in the Afternoon*
1953	*The Pleasure Garden*
1968	*The Bed*
1969	*Nuptiae*
1970	*The Golden Positions*
1971	*This is It*
1972	*Dreamwood*
1973	*High Kukus*
1974	*Testament*
1975	*The Water Circle*
1976	*Erogeny*
1976	*Together*
1977	*Windowmobile*
1977	*Song of the Godbody*
1979	*Hermes Bird*
1981	*The Gardener of Eden*
1981	*Shaman Psalm*
1983	*Devotions*
1988	*Scattered Remains*

BIBLIOGRAPHY

1949 *The Playground*
1950 *Musical Chairs*
1955 *An Almanac for Amorists*
1957 *True & False Unicorn*
1964 *The Right Playmate*
1965 *Tidings*
1969 *High Kukus*
1971 *A Long Undressing*
1977 *Seeing the Light*
1979 *Hymns to Hermes*
1982 *Graffiti for the Johns of Heaven*
1983 *Ecstasies*
1986 *A to Z*
1988 *Hooplas: Odes for Odd Occasions*
1988 *75 Lifelines*
1990 *Special Deliveries: New and Selected Poems*
1991 *The Androgyne Journal*

CITY LIGHTS PUBLICATIONS

Angulo de, Jaime. INDIANS IN OVERALLS
Angulo de, G. & J. de Angulo. JAIME IN TAOS
Artaud, Antonin. ARTAUD ANTHOLOGY
Bataille, Georges. EROTISM: Death and Sensuality
Bataille, Georges. THE IMPOSSIBLE
Bataille, Georges. STORY OF THE EYE
Bataille, Georges. THE TEARS OF EROS
Baudelaire, Charles. TWENTY PROSE POEMS
Baudelaire, Charles. INTIMATE JOURNALS
Bowles, Paul. A HUNDRED CAMELS IN THE COURTYARD
Broughton, James. MAKING LIGHT OF IT
Brown, Rebecca. THE TERRIBLE GIRLS
Bukowski, Charles. THE MOST BEAUTIFUL WOMAN IN TOWN
Bukowski, Charles. NOTES OF A DIRTY OLD MAN
Bukowski, Charles. TALES OF ORDINARY MADNESS
Burroughs, William S. THE BURROUGHS FILE
Burroughs, William S. THE YAGE LETTERS
Cassady, Neal. THE FIRST THIRD
Choukri, Mohamed. FOR BREAD ALONE
CITY LIGHTS REVIEW #1: Politics and Poetry issue
CITY LIGHTS REVIEW #2: AIDS & the Arts forum
CITY LIGHTS REVIEW #3: Media and Propaganda issue
CITY LIGHTS REVIEW #4: Literature / Politics / Ecology
Cocteau, Jean. THE WHITE BOOK (LE LIVRE BLANC)
Codrescu, Andrei, ed. EXQUISITE CORPSE READER
Cornford, Adam. ANIMATIONS
Corso, Gregory. GASOLINE
Daumal, Réne. THE POWERS OF THE WORD
David-Neel, Alexandra. SECRET ORAL TEACHINGS IN TIBETAN BUDDHIST SECTS
Deleuze, Gilles. SPINOZA: Practical Philosophy
Dick, Leslie. WITHOUT FALLING
di Prima, Diane. PIECES OF A SONG: Selected Poems
H. D. (Hilda Doolittle). NOTES ON THOUGHT & VISION
Ducornet, Rikki. ENTERING FIRE
Duras, Marguerite. DURAS BY DURAS
Eidus, Janice. VITO LOVES GERALDINE
Eberhardt, Isabelle. THE OBLIVION SEEKERS
Ferlinghetti, Lawrence. PICTURES OF THE GONE WORLD
Ferlinghetti, Lawrence. SEVEN DAYS IN NICARAGUA LIBRE
Finley, Karen. SHOCK TREATMENT
Ford, Charles Henri. OUT OF THE LABYRINTH: Selected Poems
Franzen, Cola, transl. POEMS OF ARAB ANDALUSIA
García Lorca, Federico. BARBAROUS NIGHTS: Legends & Plays
García Lorca, Federico. ODE TO WALT WHITMAN & OTHER POEMS
García Lorca, Federico. POEM OF THE DEEP SONG
Ginsberg, Allen. HOWL & OTHER POEMS
Ginsberg, Allen. KADDISH & OTHER POEMS
Ginsberg, Allen. REALITY SANDWICHES
Ginsberg, Allen. PLANET NEWS
Ginsberg, Allen. THE FALL OF AMERICA
Ginsberg, Allen. MIND BREATHS
Ginsberg, Allen. PLUTONIAN ODE

Goethe, J. W. von. TALES FOR TRANSFORMATION
Hayton-Keeva, Sally, ed. VALIANT WOMEN IN WAR AND EXILE
Herron, Don. THE DASHIELL HAMMETT TOUR: A Guidebook
Herron, Don. THE LITERARY WORLD OF SAN FRANCISCO
Higman, Perry, tr. LOVE POEMS FROM SPAIN AND SPANISH AMERICA
Jaffe, Harold. EROS: Anti-Eros
Jenkins, Edith. AGAINST A FIELD SINISTER
Kerouac, Jack. BOOK OF DREAMS
Kerouac, Jack. POEMS ALL SIZES
Kerouac, Jack. SCATTERED POEMS
Lacarrière, Jacques. THE GNOSTICS
La Duke, Betty. COMPANERAS: Women, Art & Social Change in Latin America
La Loca. ADVENTURES ON THE ISLE OF ADOLESCENCE
Lamantia, Philip. MEADOWLARK WEST
Lamantia, Philip. BECOMING VISIBLE
Laughlin, James. SELECTED POEMS: 1935-1985
Le Brun, Annie. SADE: On the Brink of the Abyss
Lowry, Malcolm. SELECTED POEMS
Marcelin, Philippe-Thoby. THE BEAST OF THE HAITIAN HILLS
Masereel, Frans. PASSIONATE JOURNEY
Mayakovsky, Vladimir. LISTEN! EARLY POEMS
Mrabet, Mohammed. THE BOY WHO SET THE FIRE
Mrabet, Mohammed. THE LEMON
Mrabet, Mohammed. LOVE WITH A FEW HAIRS
Mrabet, Mohammed. M'HASHISH
Murguia, A. & B. Paschke, eds. VOLCAN: Poems from Central America
Paschke, B. & D. Volpendesta, eds. CLAMOR OF INNOCENCE
Pessoa, Fernando. ALWAYS ASTONISHED
Peters, Nancy J., ed. WAR AFTER WAR (City Lights Review #5)
Pasolini, Pier Paolo. ROMAN POEMS
Poe, Edgar Allan. THE UNKNOWN POE
Porta, Antonio. KISSES FROM ANOTHER DREAM
Purdy, James. THE CANDLES OF YOUR EYES
Purdy, James. IN A SHALLOW GRAVE
Purdy, James. GARMENTS THE LIVING WEAR
Prévert, Jacques. PAROLES
Rachlin, Nahid. VEILS: SHORT STORIES
Rey-Rosa, Rodrigo. THE BEGGAR'S KNIFE
Rigaud, Milo. SECRETS OF VOODOO
Saadawi El, Nawal. MEMOIRS OF A WOMAN DOCTOR
Sawyer-Lauçanno, Christopher, transl. THE DESTRUCTION OF THE JAGUAR
Sclauzero, Mariarosa. MARLENE
Serge, Victor. RESISTANCE
Shepard, Sam. MOTEL CHRONICLES
Shepard, Sam. FOOL FOR LOVE & THE SAD LAMENT OF PECOS BILL
Smith, Michael. IT A COME
Snyder, Gary. THE OLD WAYS
Solnit, Rebecca. SECRET EXHIBITION: Six California Artists of the Cold War Era
Sussler, Betsy, ed. BOMB: INTERVIEWS
Takahashi, Mutsuo. SLEEPING SINNING FALLING
Turyn, Anne, ed. TOP TOP STORIES
Tutuola, Amos. FEATHER WOMAN OF THE JUNGLE
Tutuola, Amos. SIMBI & THE SATYR OF THE DARK JUNGLE
Valaoritis, Nanos. MY AFTERLIFE GUARANTEED
Wilson, Colin. POETRY AND MYSTICISM